BTEC Level 3 National Study Skills Guide in Public Services

Welcome to your Study Skills Guide! You can make it your own – start by adding your personal and course details below...

Learner's name: _____

BTEC course title: _____

Date started: _____

Mandatory units:

_____

_____

_____

Optional units:

_____

_____

_____

_____

Centre name: _____

Centre address:

_____

_____

_____

Tutor's name: _____

Published by Pearson Education Limited, a company incorporated in England and Wales, having its registered office at Edinburgh Gate, Harlow, Essex, CM20 2JE. Registered company number: 872828

Edexcel is a registered trademark of Edexcel Limited

Text © Pearson Education Limited 2010

First published 2010

16   15   14

10 9 8

British Library Cataloguing in Publication Data

A catalogue record for this book is available from the British Library

ISBN 978 1 84690 555 1

Typeset and edited by Sparks Publishing Services Ltd
Cover design by Visual Philosophy, created by EMC Design
Cover photo/illustration © Shutterstock: Monkey Business Images
Printed and bound by L.E.G.O. S.p.A. Lavis (TN) - Italy

Acknowledgements

The author and publisher would like to thank the following individuals and organisations for permission to reproduce photographs:

Alamy Images: Angela Hampton Picture Library 19, Claudia Wiens 64; **Corbis:** 74; **Getty Images:** Daniel Berehulak 15; **iStockphoto:** Chris Schmidt 33; **Pearson Education Ltd:** Steve Shott 28, Ian Wedgewood 57; **Photolibrary.com:** Image Source 82; **Reuters:** Darren Staples 10

Cover images: *Front:* **Shutterstock:** Monkey Business Images

All other images © Pearson Education

Every effort has been made to contact copyright holders of material reproduced in this book. Any omissions will be rectified in subsequent printings if notice is given to the publishers.

Websites

Go to www.pearsonhotlinks.co.uk to gain access to the relevant website links and information on how they can aid your studies. When you access the site, search for either the title BTEC Level 3 National Study Skills Guide in Public Services or ISBN 9781846905551.

Disclaimer

This material has been published on behalf of Edexcel and offers high-quality support for the delivery of Edexcel qualifications.

This does not mean that the material is essential to achieve any Edexcel qualification, nor does it mean that it is the only suitable material available to support any Edexcel qualification. Edexcel material will not be used verbatim in setting any Edexcel examination or assessment. Any resource lists produced by Edexcel shall include this and other appropriate resources.

Copies of official specifications for all Edexcel qualifications may be found on the Edexcel website: www.edexcel.com

Contents

Introduction: Ten steps to success in your BTEC Level 3 National   5

Step One: Understand your course and how it works   9

Step Two: Understand how you are assessed and graded   17

Step Three: Understand yourself   21

Step Four: Use your time wisely   25

Step Five: Utilise all your resources   31

Step Six: Understand your assessment   35

Step Seven: Work productively as a member of a group   55

Step Eight: Understand how to research and analyse information   61

Step Nine: Make an effective presentation   73

Step Ten: Maximise your opportunities and manage your problems   79

Skills building   83

Answers   93

Useful terms   95

Popular progression pathways

General qualification	Vocationally related qualification	Applied qualification
Undergraduate Degree	BTEC Higher National	Foundation Degree
GCE AS and A level	BTEC National	Advanced Diploma

Ten steps to success in your BTEC Level 3 National

This Study Skills Guide has been written to help you achieve the best result possible on your BTEC Level 3 National course. At the start of a new course you may feel both quite excited but also a little apprehensive. Taking a BTEC Level 3 National qualification has many benefits and is a major stepping stone towards your future career. Using this Study Skills Guide will help you get the most out of your course from the start.

During **induction** sessions at the start of your course, your tutor will explain important

TOP TIP

Use this Study Skills Guide at your own pace. Dip in to find what you need. Look back at it whenever you have a problem or query.

information, but it can be difficult to remember everything and that's when you'll find this Study Skills Guide invaluable. Look at it whenever you want to check anything related to your course. It provides all the essential facts you need and has a Useful terms section to explain specialist terms, words and phrases, including some that you will see highlighted in this book in bold type.

This Study Skills Guide covers the skills you'll need to do well in your course – such as managing your time, researching and analysing information and preparing a presentation.

- Use the **Top tips** to make your life easier as you go.
- Use the **Key points** to help you to stay focused on the essentials.
- Use the **Action points** to check what you need to know or do now.
- Use the **Case studies** to relate information to your chosen sector and vocational area.
- Use the **Activities** to test your knowledge and skills.
- Use the **Useful terms** section to check the meaning of specialist terms.

This Study Skills Guide has been designed to work alongside the Edexcel Student Book for BTEC Level 3 National Public Services (Edexcel, 2010). This Student Book includes the main knowledge you'll need, with tips from BTEC experts, Edexcel assignment tips, assessment activities and up-to-date case studies from industry experts, plus handy references to your Study Skills Guide.

This Study Skills Guide is divided into ten steps, each relating to a key aspect of your studies, from understanding assessment to time management to maximising opportunities. Concentrate on getting things right one step at a time. Thousands of learners have achieved BTEC Level 3 National qualifications and are now studying for a degree, or building a successful career at work. Using this Study Skills Guide, and believing in your own abilities, will help you achieve your future goals, too.

Introduction to the public sector

The public services sector is a huge area of employment. Hundreds of different organisations make up the public sector and there are thousands of job roles within these organisations. The Office of National Statistics estimates that in 2009 there were over six million people employed by the public sector.

Look around your area and consider what our public services do for us. Who do you go to if you are ill? Who do you call in an emergency? Who organises your local sports facilities or pool? Who runs your local library? What would you do if you had your mobile phone or wallet stolen? Without the public services our lives would be very different.

It is important to remember that public services are not just the emergency and armed services, which are highly visible to us. They could not operate without a huge number of civilian support workers who assist them in providing the services we often take for granted.

In the event of a major incident such as a terrorist bombing or severe flooding the public services all work together to protect lives and property. Listed below are some of the services that could be involved in a terrorist incident. Can you think of any more? Add your ideas to the list.

- Police Service
- Firefighters
- Paramedics
- Territorial Army
- Local Council
- Victim support.

Generally the public services are considered to fall into two categories: uniformed and non-uniformed. The following table shows examples of these:

Uniformed	Non-uniformed
Police Service	Probation Service
Fire and Rescue Service	Social Services
Prison Service	Education Service
HM Coastguard	Local Government
Royal Navy	Youth and Community Services
Royal Air Force	Intelligence Services
National Health Service	Mountain Rescue
Ambulance Service	The Courts Service
British Transport Police	

The interesting thing is that many services can fall into more than one category, for example most nurses wear uniform but many doctors do not. Mountain and Cave Rescue may not wear a uniform but sometimes have to perform similar rescue work to the Fire Service.

These days all the organisations listed above work together closely. This is called a 'multi-agency approach' and it is important for the success of the services. No single service can tackle society's problems on its own, which is why working in partnership is such a good idea. It means the services can share their knowledge and resources to combat the problems the public are most concerned about.

Activity:

In your opinion what are the problems the public are most concerned about?

Skills for your sector

A variety of skills are needed to be successful in the public service sector, some of which can be very difficult to learn and some of which you may already have. The BTEC Level 3 National in Public Services will help you enhance the skills you already have and develop those which you aren't quite so good at yet.

Communication Skills

Verbal communication

In the public services you will be in constant verbal communication with colleagues, superiors, members of the public and other services. It is essential that your tone and clarity of speech is good. You may need to project your voice to a crowd or speak softly to a victim of crime; you may need to speak firmly and confidently to a rowdy gang or very clearly to someone who is hard of hearing. The skill is choosing which type of verbal communication is appropriate for each situation, as choosing the wrong type could lead to a situation becoming worse instead of better.

Non-verbal communication

Your body language can tell another person a great deal about you. In fact it is estimated that about 80 per cent of all the information we receive from another person comes from their body language rather than their speech. Controlling your body language and thinking about gesture, facial expressions, posture and use of eye contact are essential skills for those working in the public sector. For example, an army officer must show confident body language when leading a mission or the team might lose confidence in their ability.

Listening

This is a vital skill across all public services. You need to listen to orders you are given, and what the public may have to say to you so you are able to act on the information you receive. If you are taking a statement from someone you will have to ask the right questions but, perhaps even more importantly, you will also have to listen very carefully to the answers. You may think you already know how to listen, but how many times have you interrupted someone while they were speaking or misunderstood instructions you have been given? The public services require 'active listeners'. This can be summarised as listening with a purpose. It involves paying attention to what is being said and questioning the speaker to ensure real understanding has been achieved. Active listening requires as much energy as speaking and it is a skill that requires practice and development if it is to be perfected.

Written communication and reading

Although the public services may look very glamorous on TV, the reality is that some of your time will be taken up with paperwork and reading documents. This part of the job may involve writing emails, internal memos and reports, taking notes, and skimming, scanning or reading documents in detail. These tasks require you to have a good standard of written English and be able to read fluently. Many of the services use reading and writing tests as part of their interview processes, so improving these skills is essential.

Teamwork

Cooperation

You will be working alongside individuals of all ages, races, religions and nationalities. You must be able to work in cooperation with all of these different people if you are going to be successful. Can you leave your prejudices behind? What if you had a personality clash with a colleague – could you still work with them successfully? Public service cooperation is called 'collaborative working'. It is very important because uniformed and non-uniformed services have to work together on a variety of tasks such as major incident response and child protection.

Leadership

There may be times you are placed into a leadership position, particularly as your career progresses. Leadership is not an easy skill to learn – it requires confidence and knowledge. Good leaders can make the difference between the success and failure of a team so this skill is very important to the public services.

Problem solving

Problem-solving abilities are essential in any job role, but they are particularly important to the public services. Many primary roles involve solving problems, such as how to move a casualty to hospital, how to stop a prison riot, where to house refugees or how to solve a crime.

Commitment

You must be able to demonstrate commitment and dedication, both to join the services in the first place and to ensure you stay in the services. Service work is challenging and often exhausting. It is not a job you can do with a half-hearted attitude: you must be prepared to work long hours and do difficult tasks.

Personal skills

Discipline

Discipline in the public services is very different from the kind of discipline you may face in other careers. Self-discipline is a really useful skill; this is where you are able to monitor and control your own conduct and behaviour. You will also need to be disciplined in your timekeeping. The way you present yourself, including the pride you take in your appearance, is also key. The public services demand high standards of personal conduct, so if this isn't a strength of yours it might be time to consider improving it.

Fitness

Fitness is really important as most uniformed public services have a physical fitness test that you have to pass to get a job. Also being physically fit helps you cope with the stress and pressure you will come under during your day-to-day work. The BTEC Level 2 First Diploma has a fitness unit built in as a core element of the course.

Decision making

The nature of public service work means that sometimes you have to make on-the-spot decisions. The Public Service Skills unit of your course will help you develop this skill.

Risk assessment

Firefighters don't rush into a burning building, police officers don't immediately remove victims from car accidents and the armed services do not rush into conflict. They assess the situation first. An injured firefighter can't save anyone! The skill of assessing the risk before you act is essential in service life.

Compassion

Many people think the services are a macho environment, but this has changed significantly over the last 20 years. You may be dealing with the most vulnerable sections of society – people who are injured, scared, unable to communicate or have lost a loved one. You will need to treat such people with kindness and compassion.

Trustworthiness

This is a key aspect of the public services. The public must be able to trust you, quite possibly with their lives, and the lives of your colleagues may also be in your hands.

Reliability

Being reliable means ensuring you are where you are supposed to be, when you are supposed to be there, doing exactly what you are supposed to do. In an emergency service call-out, if you don't get to the location on time, lives or property might be at risk.

Courage

Some situations faced by emergency and armed services will draw on all your courage. Facing the unexpected and dealing with it successfully on your course will help you learn this ability.

Regardless of the public services career you want to join there are some essential **Personal, Learning and Thinking Skills** that you will develop while you are completing your BTEC programme. See page 83 for more information on these.

Step One: Understand your course and how it works

Case study: Finding out more

Kyle, Josh and Jamilla are all planning to progress to a BTEC National in Public Services after they leave school. Each of them wants to work in a different field of the public services: Kyle wants to be a customs and revenue officer, Josh wants to work for the prison service and Jamilla wants to be a scenes of crime officer in the police service. In order to find out more about the BTEC National they agree to do some research and meet up to share what they have found out.

Kyle speaks to his local further education college. The public services tutor explains that the Public Services nationals are made up of three different awards: the National Award is six units, the National Certificate is 12 units and the National Diploma is 18 units. The tutor also explains that you can progress from the Award to the Certificate to the Diploma very easily, making the course very flexible around your needs.

Josh speaks to his schools careers adviser. The adviser tells him that the Nationals are an excellent choice for him as they are job-related qualifications, which will still allow him entry to higher education at college or university. Josh also finds out that the Nationals are equivalent to A levels. The Award is equivalent to one A level, the Certificate to two and the Diploma to three.

Jamilla speaks with her friend Matt, who is already on his second year of a BTEC National Diploma at a local college. Matt tells her that he is combining his National Diploma with an A level in PE as he wants to complete a sports science degree at university and then join the Royal Marines as an officer. Jamilla discovers that Matt is assessed mainly through coursework and many aspects of the assessments are practical.

Kyle, Josh and Jamilla meet up to share what they have found, they discover that:

1 It's possible to do a National Award, Certificate or Diploma in Public Services.

2 It's easy to transfer from one course to another if you decide to learn more.

3 They can get you entry to higher education at college or university.

4 The courses are work related and have lots of practical activities.

Reflection points

What do you think the advantages are of doing a work-based qualification?

Jamilla wants to be a scenes of crime officer. What do you think would be a good qualification to pair up with a National Certificate in Public Services?

All BTEC Level 3 National qualifications are **vocational** or **work-related**. This means that you gain specific knowledge and understanding relevant to your chosen area. It gives you several advantages when you start work.

For example, you will already know quite a lot about your chosen area, which will help you settle down more quickly. If you are already employed, you become more valuable to your employer.

Your BTEC course will prepare you for the work you want to do.

There are four types of BTEC Level 3 National qualification: Certificates, Subsidiary Diplomas, Diplomas and Extended Diplomas

	Certificate	Subsidiary Diploma	Diploma	Extended Diploma
Credit	30	60	120	180
Equivalence	1 AS-level	1 A-level	2 A-levels	3 A-levels

These qualifications are often described as **nested**. This means that they fit inside each other (rather like Russian dolls) because the same units are common to each qualification – so you can progress from one to another easily by completing more units.

TOP TIP

The structure of BTEC Level 3 National qualifications means it's easy to progress from one type to another and gain more credits, as well as specialise in particular areas that interest you.

- Every BTEC Level 3 National qualification has a set number of **mandatory units** that all learners must complete.
- All BTEC Level 3 National qualifications include **optional units** that enable you to study particular areas in more depth.

- Some BTEC Level 3 National qualifications have **specialist pathways**, which may have additional mandatory units. These specialist pathways allow you to follow your career aims more precisely. For example, if you are studying to become an IT practitioner, you can choose pathways in Software Development, Networking, Systems Support or IT and Business.

- On all BTEC courses you are expected to be responsible for your own learning. Obviously your tutor will give you help and guidance when necessary but you also need to be 'self-starting' and able to use your own initiative. Ideally, you can also assess how well you are doing and make improvements when necessary.

- BTEC Level 3 National grades convert to UCAS points, just like A-levels, but the way you are assessed and graded on a BTEC course is different, as you will see in the next section.

Key points

- You can study part-time or full-time for your BTEC Level 3 National.

- You can do a Certificate, Subsidiary Diploma, Diploma, or Extended Diploma, and progress easily from one to the other.

- You will study both mandatory units and optional units on your course.

- When you have completed your BTEC course you can get a job (or **apprenticeship**), use your qualification to develop your career and/or continue studying to degree level.

- On all BTEC Level 3 National courses, the majority of your learning is practical and vocationally focused to develop the skills you need for your chosen career.

Using the Edexcel website to find out about your course

- You can check all the details about your BTEC Level 3 National course on the Edexcel website – go to www.edexcel.com.

- Enter the title of your BTEC Level 3 National qualification in the qualifications finder.

- Now find the specification in the list of documents. This is a long document so don't try to print it. Instead, look at the information on the units you will be studying to see the main topics you will cover.

- Then save the document or bookmark the page so that you can easily refer to it again if you need to.

Action points

1 By discussing with your tutor and by exploring the Edexcel website, find out the key information about your course and use it to complete the 'Important Information' form on the next page. You can refer to this form at any time to refresh your memory about any part of your studies.

a) Check whether you are studying for a BTEC Level 3 Certificate, Subsidiary Diploma, Diploma, or Extended Diploma and the number of units you will be studying.

b) Find out the titles of the mandatory units you will be studying.

c) Find out the titles of the optional units and identify the ones offered at your centre.

d) Check the length of your course, and when you will be studying each unit.

e) Identify the optional units you will be taking. On some National courses you will do this at the start, while on others you may make your final decision later.

f) Find out other relevant information about your BTEC Level 3 National qualification. Your centre may have already given you details about the structure.

g) Ask your tutor to help you to complete point 10 on the form. Depending on your course, you may be developing specific additional or personal skills – such as personal, learning and thinking skills (PLTS) and functional skills – or spending time on work experience, going on visits or doing other activities linked to your subject area.

h) Talk to your tutor about point 12 on the form as your sources of information will depend on the careers guidance and information at your centre. You may find it useful to exchange ideas with other members of your class.

IMPORTANT INFORMATION ON MY BTEC LEVEL 3 NATIONAL COURSE	
1	The title of the BTEC Level 3 National qualification I am studying is:
2	The length of my course is:
3	The total number of units I will study is:
4	The number of mandatory units I have to study is:
5	The titles of these mandatory units and the dates (or terms) when I will study them are:
6	The main topics I will learn in each mandatory unit include:

	IMPORTANT INFORMATION ON MY BTEC LEVEL 3 NATIONAL COURSE
7	The number of optional units I have to study is:
8	The titles of the optional units I will study are:
9	The main topics I will learn in each optional unit include:
10	Other important aspects of my course are:
11	After I have achieved my BTEC Level 3 National my options include:
12	Useful sources of information I can use to find out more about these options include:

2 Many learners already have information, contacts or direct experiences that relate to their course. For example, you may have a specific interest or hobby that links to a unit, such as being a St John Ambulance cadet if you are studying Public Services. Think about the relevant sources of information you already have access to and complete the table below.

MY INFORMATION SOURCES	
Experts I know	(Who they are, what they know)
My hobbies and interests	(What they are, what they involve)
My job(s)	(Past and present work and work experience, and what I did)
Programmes I like to watch	(What these are, how they relate to my course)
Magazines and/or books I read	(What these are, examples of relevant articles)
ICT sources	(My centre's intranet as well as useful websites)
Other	(Other sources relevant for my particular course and the topics I will be studying)

Volunteering may help you to understand more about how public services operate.

Activity: Your future options

At the beginning of a new course it is helpful to think about what options may be available to you for your career pathway in health and social care. All assignments and work experience on the programme contribute to your final grade and knowing what you are aiming for will help keep you motivated.

Using a mind map to explore different ideas is a way for you to start to consider the range of options available to you and what you will need to follow each career pathway.

For example, if you wish to work with the community, you could explore the different routes to becoming a police community support officer (PCSO).

You will find the internet a useful source of information. A good starting point is the police service recruitment website. Go to page 94 to find out how to access this link.

Create a mind map on the next page to record your ideas.

TOP TIP

People usually perform better if they understand why they have chosen, or been asked, to do something.

Career options available
to me in Public Services

Step Two: Understand how you are assessed and graded

Case study: Assignments and grading; Maura's experience

'I didn't do a BTEC First, so when I came on the National Diploma I didn't really have any idea how I would be assessed or graded. I had done GCSEs at school and I knew about coursework and exams, but what I did at school was very different to the work I have had to do on my BTEC National Diploma in Public Services.

The first thing that was different was the assignments. Sometimes you might get a big assignment that covers a whole unit and sometimes you might get a few smaller assignments covering a unit. The assignments can be really varied from practical assessments, presentations, posters, leaflets, reports, essays or worksheets. This is good because you don't get bored just doing the same thing over and over and it lets you try things that you might not have done before.

My favourite assignment this year was for my *International Perspectives* unit. We had to work in small groups to produce a documentary on terrorism. I hadn't done anything like it before but it really built my confidence and my team made a really professional documentary which was shown to the whole year group.

The grading is different too. At school I was used to getting A, B, C, etc. but on a National the grading is at pass, merit and distinction level. The really cool thing about this is that the assignments tell you exactly what you need to do to get each grade; you are not left to work it out for yourself. So I've found my grades on the National Diploma have really improved compared to my school work. I always pay special attention to any questions on my assignments which are labelled merit or distinction. Good grades are really important to me as I want to go and do a law degree after college and I need 360 UCAS points to get into the best universities, so I'm aiming for distinctions where I can.'

Reflection points

Maura talks about the variety of assessment methods used on the BTEC National course. Think about all of the types of assessment she lists:

practical assessments; presentations; posters; leaflets; reports; essays; worksheets.

- Which types of assessment do you think you might be best at?
- How do these assessment methods make use of your strengths?
- Which ones do you think you might find more difficult?
- What could you do to make these types of assessment easier to tackle?

Your assessment

This section looks at the importance of your assignments, how they are graded and how this converts into unit points and UCAS points. Unlike A-levels, there are no externally-set final exams on a BTEC course. Even if you know this because you already have a BTEC First qualification, you should still read this section as now you will be working at a different level.

Your learning is assessed by **assignments**, set by your tutors. You will complete these throughout your course, using many different **assessment methods**, such as real-life case studies, **projects** and presentations. Some assignments may be work-based or **time-constrained** – it depends very much on the vocational area you are studying.

Your assignments are based on **learning outcomes** set by Edexcel. These are listed for each unit in your course specification. You must achieve **all** the learning outcomes to pass each unit.

TOP TIP

Check the learning outcomes for each unit by referring to the course specification – go to www.edexcel.com.

Important skills to help you achieve your grades include:

- researching and analysing information (see page 61)
- using your time effectively (see page 25)
- working co-operatively as a member of a team (see page 55.)

Your grades, unit points and UCAS points

On a BTEC Level 3 National course, assessments that meet the learning outcomes are graded as pass, merit or distinction. The different grades within each unit are set out by Edexcel as **grading criteria** in a **grading grid**. These criteria identify

the **higher-level skills** you must demonstrate to achieve a higher grade (see also Step Six – Understand your assessment, on page 35).

All your assessment grades earn **unit points**. The total points you get for all your units determines your final qualification grade(s) – pass, merit or distinction. You get:

- one final grade if you are taking a Certificate or Subsidiary Diploma
- two final grades if you are taking a Diploma
- three final grades if you are taking an Extended Diploma.

Your points and overall grade(s) convert to **UCAS points**, which you need to be accepted onto a degree course. For example, if you achieve three final pass grades for your BTEC Level 3 Extended Diploma, you get 120 UCAS Tariff points. If you achieve three final distinction grades, this increases to 360 – equivalent to three GCE A-levels.

Please note that all UCAS information was correct at the time of going to print, but we would advise that you check their website for the most up to date information. See page 94 for how to access their website.

 Case study: Securing a university place

Chris and Shaheeda both want a university place and have worked hard on their BTEC Level 3 Extended Diploma course.

Chris's final score is 226 unit points, which converts to 280 UCAS Tariff points. Shaheeda has a total score of 228 unit points – just two points more – which converts to 320 UCAS points! This is because a score of between 204 and 227 unit points gives 280 UCAS points, whereas a score of 228 to 251 points gives 320 UCAS points.

Shaheeda is delighted because this increases her chances of getting a place on the degree course she wants. Chris is annoyed. He says if he had realised he would have worked harder on his last assignment to get two points more.

You start to earn points from your first assessment, so you get many benefits from settling in quickly and doing good work from the start. Understanding how **grade boundaries** work also helps you to focus your efforts to get the best possible final grade.

You will be able to discuss your learning experiences, your personal progress and the

achievement of your learning objectives in **individual tutorials** with your tutor. These enable you to monitor your progress and overcome temporary difficulties. You can also talk about any worries you have. Your tutor is one of your most important resources and a tutorial gives you their undivided attention.

You can talk through any questions or problems in your tutorials.

Key points

- Your learning is assessed in a variety of ways, such as by assignments, projects and real-life case studies.

- You need to demonstrate specific knowledge and skills to achieve the learning outcomes set by Edexcel. You must achieve all the grading criteria to pass a unit.

- The grading criteria for pass, merit and distinction are shown in a grading grid for the unit. Higher-level skills are needed for higher grades.

- The assessment grades of pass, merit and distinction convert to unit points. The total unit points you receive for the course determines your final overall grade(s) and UCAS points.

TOP TIP

It's always tempting to spend longer on work you like doing and are good at, but focusing on improving your weak areas will do more to boost your overall grade(s).

Action points

1 Find out more about your own course by carrying out this activity.

   a) Find the learning outcomes for the units you are currently studying. Your tutor may have given you these, or you can find them in your course specification – go to www.edexcel.com and search for your qualification.

   b) Look at the grading grid for the units and identify the way the requirements change for the higher grades. If there are some unfamiliar words, check these in Step Six of this guide (see page 35 onwards).

   c) If the unit points system still seems complicated, ask your tutor to explain it.

   d) Check the UCAS points you would need for the course or university which interests you.

   e) Design a form you can use to record the unit points you earn throughout your course. Keep this up-to-date. Regularly check how your points relate to your overall grade(s), based on the grade boundaries for your qualification. Your tutor can give you this information or you can check it yourself in the course specification.

Activity: Researching assessment and grading

Finding out how your course is assessed, and how you will be graded, will play a key part in how well you perform on your BTEC National in Public Services. This activity requires you to do some research into how your particular centre will assess and grade you:

1 Speak with your tutor and describe all the types of assessments you will be doing in your first set of assignments.

2 Which of these assignments are linked to pass grades?

3 Which of these assignments are linked to merit and distinction grades?

4 What are your tutor's top tips for achieving merit and distinction grades?

Step Three: Understand yourself

Case study: Being self-aware; Wu Xia's experience

'As part of our induction on to the National Certificate in Public Services we had to do a personality test. The whole class did it, and the tutor joined in and did hers as well. It was meant to be a bit of fun so that we could see what personality types we had and so we could see who had the same personality types as we did. The tutor explained that not only would she get to know a bit more about us before we started the course, but we could get to know a bit more about ourselves and our colleagues as well. This would help us in making new friends and study groups.

I actually found the test really useful. It was challenging to answer some of the questions honestly like about our strengths and weaknesses, but it really gave me an insight into why I do certain things and why certain things annoy me more than others. It was also really useful to see what approach we might take to our studies. The personality test showed me as being quite disorganised and with a weakness in time management. I know this is true because I'm always struggling to find things and I always leave assignments and jobs until the last minute before I start them. It also said that I worry easily and this might distract me from my work.

One of the good things about doing this test is that I now have a clear idea of what might trip me up on my course: I need to be more organised and start tasks on time; I also need to make sure that if I start to worry about my course I keep calm and see my tutor if required. Completing these tests was also a really useful exercise for Unit 16 – Career Planning for the Uniformed Public Services – as I was able to assess my personal skills against what the services are looking for.'

Reflection points

Which of your personal qualities do you think will be useful on the National in Public Services?

What do you think will be your main weaknesses on the course?

How can you try and overcome your weaknesses?

How do you prefer to study, independently? With others? A quiet environment? A busy environment? Consider how your preferences might affect how successful you are in your studies.

Self-awareness means understanding how you 'tick'. For example, do you prefer practical activities rather than theory? Do you prefer to draw or sketch an idea, rather than write about it?

Self-awareness is important as it makes you less reliant on other people's opinions and gives you confidence in your own judgement. You can also reflect on your actions to learn from your experiences.

Self-awareness also means knowing your own strengths and weaknesses. Knowing your strengths enables you to feel positive and confident about yourself and your abilities. Knowing your weaknesses means you know the areas you need to develop.

You can analyse yourself by looking at...

... your personality and preferences

You may have taken a personality test at your centre. If not, your tutor may recommend one to use, or there are many available online.

Many employers ask job candidates to complete a personality test so that they can match the type of work they are offering to the most suitable candidates. Although these tests can only give a broad indication of someone's personality they may help to avoid mismatches, such as hiring someone who is introverted to work in sales.

... your skills and abilities

To succeed in your assignments, and to progress in a career, requires a number of skills. Some may be vocationally-specific, or professional, skills that you can improve during your course – such as sporting performance on a Sports course. Others are broader skills that are invaluable no matter what you are studying – such as communicating clearly and co-operating with others.

You will work faster and more accurately, and have greater confidence, if you are skilled and proficient. A quick skills check will identify any problem areas.

TOP TIP

Use the Skills Building section on page 83 to identify the skills you need for your course. You'll also find hints and tips for improving any weak areas.

Key points

- You need certain skills and abilities to get the most out of your BTEC Level 3 National course and to develop your career potential.
- Knowing your strengths and weaknesses is a sign of maturity. It gives you greater confidence in your abilities and enables you to focus on areas for improvement.

TOP TIP

You will find more help on developing your skills and abilities in the sections on: Working as a member of a group; Using time wisely; Researching and analysing information; and Making effective presentations.

Action points

1 Gain insight into your own personality by answering each of the following statements *True* or *False* with a tick. Be honest!

		True	False
a)	If someone annoys me, I can tell them about it without causing offence.		
b)	If someone is talking, I often interrupt them to give them my opinion.		
c)	I get really stressed if I'm under pressure.		
d)	I can sometimes become very emotional and upset on other people's behalf.		
e)	I sometimes worry that I can't cope and may make a mess of something.		
f)	I am usually keen, enthusiastic and motivated to do well.		
g)	I enjoy planning and organising my work.		
h)	I find it easy to work and co-operate with other people and take account of their opinions.		
i)	I am easily influenced by other people.		
j)	I often jump to conclusions and judge people and situations on first impressions.		
k)	I prefer to rely on facts and experience rather than following my instincts.		

Now identify which of the skills and qualities in the box below will be really important in your chosen career.

> tact   truthfulness   listening skills
>
> staying calm under pressure
>
> empathy with others   self-confidence
>
> initiative   planning and organising
>
> working with others   self-assurance
>
> objective judgements

Use your answers to identify areas you should work on to be successful in the future.

2 As part of the UCAS process, all **higher education** applicants have to write a personal statement. This is different from a CV, which is a summary of achievements that all job applicants prepare. You may have already prepared a CV but not thought about a personal statement. Now is your chance to!

Read the information about personal statement in the box. Then answer these questions:

a) Explain why personal statements are so important for higher education applicants.

b) Why do you think it is important for your personal statement to read well and be error-free?

c) Suggest three reasons why you shouldn't copy a pre-written statement you have found online.

d) Check the websites you can access from the hotlink given in the box to see what to include in the statement and how to set it out.

e) Prepare a bullet point list of ten personal facts. Focus on your strengths and good reasons why you should be given a place on the higher education course of your choice. If possible, discuss your list with your tutor. Then keep it safely, as it will be useful if you need to write a personal statement later.

Personal statements

This is the information that all higher education applicants have to put in the blank space on their UCAS form. The aim is to sell yourself to admissions tutors. It can be pretty scary, especially if you haven't written anything like it before.

So, where do you start?

First, *never* copy pre-written statements you find online. These are just for guidance. Even worse are websites that offer to write your statement for a fee, and send you a few general, pre-written paragraphs. Forget them all: you can do better!

Imagine you are an admissions tutor with 60 places to offer to 200 applicants. What will you need to read in a personal statement to persuade you to offer the applicant a place?

Most likely, clear explanations about:

- what the applicant can contribute to the course
- why the applicant really wants a place on your course
- what the applicant has done to further his/her own interests in this area, eg voluntary work
- attributes that show this applicant would be a definite bonus – such as innovative ideas, with evidence eg 'I organised a newsletter which we published every three months …'

A personal statement should be well written, with no grammatical or spelling errors and organised into clear paragraphs.

There are a number of helpful websites with information on personal statements. Go to page 94 to find out how to access these sites.

Activity: Preparing your personal statement

Producing a personal statement for higher education involves knowing yourself and what motivates you really well. The person reading it should be able to see your personality shine through and they will know from reading it how well you know yourself.

Jot down notes to the following questions:

1 Why do you want to study your chosen subject?

2 What activities have you undertaken which are relevant to your course choice?

3 What are your major strengths as a learner?

4 What have you experienced in your life that has made you the person you are today?

5 What activities are you involved in outside of school or college?

6 How have these activities helped you develop as a person

7 What qualities do you have that will make you a good learner?

8 Why should they choose you over other applicants?

9 Where do you see yourself in ten years' time?

The same kind of questions can be used with any personal statement. Remember that most public service job applications are heavily paper sifted. It makes sense to have a solid personal statement ready for when you apply to HE or a public services career.

Step Four: Use your time wisely

Case study: Time management survey

For one of their units, Anya and Ruby were set the task of conducting a small survey of current second-year National Diploma in Public Service learners to see how they managed their time in their first year, and whether we could learn from the problems they encountered.

'Time management is really important because the public services often have to operate under strict time constraints such as 999 response times, so it's important that we learn these skills now. It was also really useful when looking at Unit 16 – Career Planning for the Uniformed Public Services – as time management and personal development are key parts of the content.

Our survey only had three questions:

1 Did you find managing your time a problem in your first year?
2 What were the major time-wasters you encountered?
3 What advice would you give to new first years so they can avoid the problems you had.

The results were really interesting: 100 per cent of the second years had had problems with their time management in their first year. They came up with lots of reasons why and lots of good advice for us. We put the results into tables to discuss with the rest of our class in tutorial sessions.'

Top five time-wasters
Going out with friends too often
Working too many hours in paid employment
Online activities such as Facebook
Computer games
Television

Top five pieces of advice
Start work as soon as you get it
Don't work more than 10–15 hours a week
Be organised
Work in study groups
Stay in the library after your sessions finish. Don't just go home

Reflection points

Do you recognise any of these time-wasters as distracting your from your own studies?

Think about which of these time-wasters would be most likely to distract you from your studies. Would you add any others to the list?

Do you think any of the solutions would help you manage your time more effectively?

Most learners have to combine course commitments with other responsibilities such as a job (either full- or part-time) and family responsibilities. You will also want to see your friends and keep up your hobbies and interests. Juggling these successfully means you need to be able to use your time wisely.

This involves planning what to do and when to do it to prevent panics about unexpected deadlines. As your course progresses, this becomes even more important as your workload may increase towards the end of a term. In some cases there could be two or more assignments to complete simultaneously. Although tutors try to avoid clashes of this sort, it is sometimes inevitable.

To cope successfully, you need time-management skills, in particular:

* how to organise your time to be more productive
* how to prioritise tasks
* how to overcome time-wasters.

Organising your time

- **Use a diary or wall chart.**
  Using a different colour pen for each, enter:
  - your course commitments, eg assignment dates, tutorials, visits
  - important personal commitments, eg sports matches, family birthdays
  - your work commitments.

TOP TIP

A diary is useful because you can update it as you go, but a wall chart gives you a better overview of your commitments over several weeks. Keep your diary or chart up to date and check ahead regularly so that you have prior warning of important dates.

- **Identify how you currently use your time.**
  - Work out how much time you spend at your centre, at work, at home and on social activities.
  - Identify which commitments are vital and which are optional so you can find extra time if necessary.

- **Plan and schedule future commitments.**
  - Write down any appointments and tasks you must do.
  - Enter assignment review dates and final deadline dates in different colours.
  - This should stop you from arranging a dental appointment on the same morning that you are due to give an important presentation or planning a hectic social life when you have lots of course work to do.

- **Decide your best times for doing course work.**
  - Expect to do most of your course work in your own time.
  - Work at the time of day when you feel at your best.
  - Work regularly, and in relatively short bursts, rather than once or twice a week for very long stretches.
  - If you're a night owl, allow an hour to 'switch off' before you go to bed.

- **Decide where to work.**
  - Choose somewhere you can concentrate without interruption.
  - Make sure there is space for resources you use, such as books or specialist equipment.
  - You also need good lighting and a good – but not too comfortable – chair.
  - If you can't find suitable space at home, check out your local or college library.

- **Assemble the items you need.**
  - Book ahead to get specific books, journals or DVDs from the library.
  - Ensure you have your notes, handouts and assignment brief with you.
  - Use sticky notes to mark important pages in textbooks or folders.

TOP TIP

Set yourself a target when you start work, so that you feel positive and productive at the end. Always try to end a session when a task is going well, rather than when you are stuck. Then you will be keener to go back to it the next day. Note down outstanding tasks you need to continue with next time.

- **Plan ahead**
  - If anything is unclear about an assignment, ask your tutor for an explanation as soon as you can.
  - Break down long tasks or assignments into manageable chunks, eg find information, decide what to use, create a plan for finished work, write rough draft of first section, etc.
  - Work back from deadline dates so that you allow plenty of time to do the work.
  - Always allow more time than you need. It is better to finish early than to run out of time.

TOP TIP

If you are working on a task as a group, organise and agree times to work together. Make sure you have somewhere to meet where you can work without disturbing other courses or groups.

- **Be self-disciplined.**
  - Don't put things off because you're not in the mood. Make it easier by doing simple tasks first to get a sense of achievement. Then move on to something harder.
  - Plan regular breaks. If you're working hard you need a change of activity to recharge your batteries.
  - If you have a serious problem or personal crisis, talk to your personal tutor promptly.

TOP TIP

Make sure you know the consequences of missing an assignment deadline, as well as the dispensations and exemptions that can be given if you have an unavoidable and serious problem, such as illness (see also page 81).

How to prioritise tasks

Prioritising means doing the most important and urgent task first. Normally this will be the task or assignment with the closest deadline or the one that will most affect your overall course grades.

One way of prioritising is to group tasks into ABC categories.

Category A tasks	These must be done now as they are very important and cannot be delayed, eg completing an assignment to be handed in tomorrow.
Category B tasks	These are jobs you should do if you have time, because otherwise they will rapidly become Category A, eg getting a book that you need for your next assignment.
Category C tasks	These are tasks you should do if you have the time, eg rewriting notes jotted down quickly in a lesson.

Expect to be flexible. For example, if you need to allow time for information to arrive, then send for this first. If you are working in a team, take into account other people's schedules when you are making arrangements.

Avoiding time-wasters

Everyone has days when they don't know where the time has gone. It may be because they were constantly interrupted or because things just kept going wrong. Whatever the reason, the end result is that some jobs don't get done.

If this happens to you regularly, you need to take steps to keep on track.

Some useful tips are:

- **Warn people in advance when you will be working.**
  - Ask them to not interrupt you.
  - If you are in a separate room, shut the door. If someone comes in, make it clear you don't want to talk.
  - If that doesn't work, find somewhere else (or some other time) to work.
- **Switch off your mobile, TV, radio and iPod/ MP3 player.**
  - Don't respond to, or make, calls or texts.
  - If someone rings your home phone, let voicemail answer or ask them to call back later.
- **Be strict with yourself when you are working online.**
  - Don't check your email until you've finished work.
  - Don't get distracted when searching for information.
  - Keep away from social networking sites.
- **Avoid displacement activities.**
  - These are the normally tedious jobs, such as cleaning your computer screen, that suddenly seem far more attractive than working!

Talking to friends can occupy a lot of time.

TOP TIP

The first step in managing your own time is learning to say 'no' (nicely!) if someone asks you to do something tempting when you should be working.

Key points

- Being in control of your time allows you to balance your commitments according to their importance and means you won't let anyone down.
- Organising yourself and your time involves knowing how you spend your time now, planning when and where it is best to work, scheduling commitments and setting sensible timescales to complete your work.
- Knowing how to prioritise means you will schedule work effectively according to its urgency and importance. You will need self-discipline to follow the schedule you have set for yourself.
- Identifying ways in which you may waste time means you can guard against these to achieve your goals more easily.

TOP TIP

Benefits to managing your own time include being less stressed (because you are not reacting to problems or crises), producing better work and having time for a social life.

Action points

1 Start planning your time properly.

a) Find out how many assignments you will have this term, and when you will get them. Put this information into your diary or planner.

b) Update this with your other commitments for the term – both work/course-related and social. Identify possible clashes and decide how to resolve the problem.

c) Identify one major task or assignment you will do soon. Divide it into manageable chunks and decide how long to allow for each chunk, plus some spare time for any problems. If possible, check your ideas with your tutor before you put them into your planner.

2 How good are you at being responsible for your own learning?

a) Fill in the following table. Score yourself out of 5 for each area: where 0 is awful and 5 is excellent. Ask a friend or relative to score you as well. See if you can explain any differences.

	Scoring yourself	Other person's score for you
Being punctual		
Organisational ability		
Tidiness		
Working accurately		
Finding and correcting own mistakes		
Solving problems		
Accepting responsibility		
Working with details		
Planning how to do a job		
Using own initiative		
Thinking up new ideas		
Meeting deadlines		

b) Draw up your own action plan for areas where you need to improve. If possible, talk this through at your next **tutorial** (see page 98).

Activity: Planning your time

Use the planner below to plan your study time. Be sure to include:

- Your college sessions
- Your private study time
- Group study time
- Social activities
- Paid Employment
- Anything else you consider important.

Getting into a study routine is really important and will help you manage your busy life. Being organised with your time will help you to achieve your best on your BTEC National Public Services course.

	Monday	Tuesday	Wednesday	Thursday	Friday	Saturday	Sunday
8–9 am							
9–10 am							
10–11 am							
11–12 pm							
12–1 pm							
1–2 pm							
2–3 pm							
3–4 pm							
4–5 pm							
5–6 pm							
6–7 pm							
7–8 pm							

Step Five: Utilise all your resources

Case study: Using your resources

Learners from the first year National Diploma in Public Services at a South Yorkshire college formed an organised study club to run three times a week after taught sessions. The club runs in the college's library Tuesday, Wednesday and Thursday 4 pm–6 pm. The club has its own chair and secretary, and publishes a study timetable each week with details of which assignments they will focus on each evening. The chair is called Brynn and he had this to say:

'We set up the study club because we realised that many of us worked better in groups than we did on our own. It's easy to leave college straight after sessions and then get stuck with your work at home and not be able to talk to anyone about it. In the study club we are all working on the same assignment at the same time, so we can use each other's knowledge and good ideas to improve our work.

We are also in the college library so we have access to computers, books, journals and newspapers to help us. The tutors are usually here until about 6 pm too so if we get stuck we can pop to their office and ask for some advice. They have been really helpful with the club and they will often pop in to see if we are OK or if we need any help.'

Reflection points

Do you think a study club or a group would help you complete your work?

If so, how would it be helpful?

Think about how you could go about organising a study club at your centre.

Your resources are all the things that can help you to be successful in your BTEC Level 3 National qualification, from your favourite website to your study buddy (see page 32) who collects handouts for you if you miss a class.

Your centre will provide essential resources, such as a library with appropriate books and electronic reference sources, the computer network and internet access. You will have to provide basic resources such as pens, pencils and file folders yourself. If you have to buy your own textbooks, look after them carefully so you can sell them on at the end of your course.

Here is a list of resources, with tips for getting the best out of them.

- **Course information**. This includes your course specification, this Study Skills Guide and all information on the Edexcel website relating to your BTEC Level 3 National course. Course information from your centre will include term dates, assignment dates and your timetable. Keep everything safely so you can refer to it whenever you need to clarify something.

- **Course materials**. These include course handouts, printouts, your own notes and textbooks. Put handouts into an A4 folder as soon as you get them. Use a separate folder for each unit you study.

TOP TIP

Filing notes and handouts promptly means they don't get lost, will stay clean and uncrumpled and you won't waste time looking for them.

- **Stationery**. You need pens and pencils, a notepad, a hole puncher, a stapler and sets of dividers. Dividers should be clearly labelled to help you store and quickly find notes, printouts and handouts. Your notes should be headed and dated, and those from your own research must also include your source (see Step Eight – page 61 onwards.)

- **People**. Your tutors, specialist staff at college, classmates, your employer and work colleagues, your relatives and friends are all valuable resources. Many will have particular skills or work in the vocational area that you are studying. Talking to other learners can help to clarify issues that there may not have been time to discuss fully in class.

A **study buddy** is another useful resource as they can make notes and collect handouts if you miss a session. (Remember to return the favour when they are away.)

Always be polite when you are asking people for information. Prepare the questions first and remember that you are asking for help, not trying to get them to do the work for you! If you are interviewing someone for an assignment or project, good preparations are vital. (See Step Eight – page 61 onwards.)

If someone who did the course before you offers help, be careful. It is likely the course requirements will have changed. Never be tempted to copy their assignments (or someone else's). This is **plagiarism** – a deadly sin in the educational world (see also Step Six – page 35.)

TOP TIP

A positive attitude, an enquiring mind and the ability to focus on what is important will have a major impact on your final result.

Key points

- Resources help you to achieve your qualification. Find out what resources you have available to you and use them wisely.
- Have your own stationery items.
- Know how to use central facilities and resources such as the library, learning resource centres and your computer network. Always keep to the policy on IT use in your centre.
- People are a key resource – school or college staff, work colleagues, members of your class, friends, family and people who are experts in their field.

TOP TIP

Learn to be your own best resource by developing the skills you need to work quickly and accurately.

Action points

1 a) List the resources you will need to complete your course successfully. Identify which ones will be provided by your school or college, and which you need to supply yourself.

   b) Go through your list again and identify the resources you already have (or know how to access) and those you don't.

   c) Compare your list with a friend's and decide how to obtain and access the resources you need. Add any items to your list that you forgot.

   d) List the items you still need to get and set a target date for doing this.

2 'Study buddy' schemes operate in many centres. Find out if this applies to your own centre and how you can make the best use of it.

In some you can choose your study buddy, in others people are paired up by their tutor.
- Being a study buddy might mean just collecting handouts when the other person is absent, and giving them important news.
- It may also mean studying together and meeting (or keeping contact by phone or email) to exchange ideas and share resources.

With a study buddy you can share resources and stay on top of the course if you're ever away.

Activity: Resources

Consider what resources you need for your public services course, use the table below to record them. One example is given for you.

Resource	How important	Where found	Cost
Public Services Textbook	Very important	Bookshop or library	Free to use in library; approx £20 for a personal copy

Step Six: Understand your assessment

Case study: Mohammed's assignment troubles

'I was really excited to get our first assignment on the Public Service course. I enjoy doing coursework and I knew I could do well as the subject was *Understanding Discipline*. This is something I think I know a lot about because I have been in the Army Cadets for three years.

I wrote as much as I could about my understanding of discipline and related it to my experience of working in the cadets. The assignment was seven pages long and I was really pleased with it. I presented it in a new document wallet and it looked really professional.

When it came back and I hadn't passed I was absolutely gutted and angry, and I couldn't understand why I hadn't even got a pass when I thought I deserved a distinction.

I went to see my tutor straight away. She asked me if I had read the feedback on the assignment. I hadn't read it as I was so sure she was wrong about my grade. She explained that reading the feedback on the assignment is really important because it tells you where you have gone wrong. The tutor talked through the feedback with me and it was clear that I actually hadn't answered the question at all.

The assignment was centred on a pass and merit criteria which cover conformity and obedience – I hadn't even mentioned them in my assignment. I was embarrassed to admit that I actually hadn't read the assignment at all. I had seen the title *Understanding Discipline* and had just written off the top of my head. Worse than that, the actual work was a presentation and I had done a report.

I learned two really important things from this. Firstly, ALWAYS read the assignment properly and make sure you are certain what you have to do before you do anything. Secondly, read the feedback from your tutor, they want you to do well and their advice is really valuable.'

Reflection points

How do think you would you feel in Mohammed's place?

Have you ever tried to complete a piece of work without fully understanding it?

What were the results?

Being successful on any BTEC Level 3 National course means first understanding what you must do in your assignments – and then doing it.

Your assignments focus on topics you have already covered in class. If you've attended regularly, you should be able to complete them confidently.

However, there are some common pitfalls it's worth thinking about. Here are tips to avoid them:

- Read the instructions (the assignment brief) properly and several times before you start.

- Make sure you understand what you are supposed to do. Ask if anything is unclear.

- Complete every part of a task. If you ignore a question, you can't meet the grading criteria.

- Prepare properly. Do your research or reading before you start. Don't guess the answers.

- Communicate your ideas clearly. You can check this by asking someone who doesn't know the subject to look at your work.

- Only include relevant information. Padding out answers makes it look as if you don't know your subject.

- Do the work earlier rather than later to avoid any last-minute panics.

- Pay attention to advice and feedback that your tutor has given you.

The assignment 'brief'

This may be longer than its name implies! The assignment brief includes all the instructions for an assignment and several other details, as you can see in the table below.

What will you find in a BTEC Level 3 National assignment brief?	
Content	**Details**
Title	This will link to the unit and learning outcomes
Format/style	Written assignment, presentation, demonstration, etc
Preparation	Read case study, do research, etc
Learning outcomes	These state the knowledge you must demonstrate to obtain a required grade
Grading criterion/ criteria covered	eg P1/M1/D1
Individual/group work	Remember to identify your own contribution in any group work
Feedback	Tutor, peer review
Interim review dates	Dates to see your tutor
Final deadline	Last submission date

Your centre's rules and regulations

Your centre will have several policies and guidelines about assignments, which you need to check carefully. Many, such as those listed below, relate to Edexcel policies and guidelines.

- The procedure to follow if you have a serious problem and can't meet a deadline. An extension may be granted.
- The penalty for missing a deadline without good reason.
- The penalty for copying someone else's work. This is usually severe, so never share your work (or CDs or USB flash drive) with anyone else, and don't borrow theirs.
- **Plagiarism** is also serious misconduct. This means copying someone's work or quoting from books and websites and pretending it is your own work.
- The procedure to follow if you disagree with the grade you are given.

Understanding the question or task

There are two aspects to a question or task. The first is the **command words**, which are described below. The second is the **presentation instructions**, which is what you are asked to do – don't write a report when you should be producing a chart!

Command words, such as 'explain', 'describe', 'analyse', 'evaluate', state how a question must be answered. You may be asked to 'describe' something at pass level, but you will need to do more, perhaps 'analyse' or 'evaluate', to achieve merit or distinction.

Many learners fail to achieve higher grades because they don't realise the difference between these words. Instead of analysing or evaluating they give an explanation instead. Adding more details won't achieve a higher grade – you need to change your whole approach to the answer.

The **grading grid** for each unit of your course gives you the command words, so that you know what to do to achieve a pass, merit or distinction. The tables that follow show you what is usually required when you see a particular command word. These are just examples to guide you as the exact response will depend on the question. If you have any doubts, check with your tutor before you start work.

There are two important points to note.

- A command word such as 'create' or 'explain' may be repeated in the grading criteria for different grades. In these cases the complexity or range of the task itself increases at the higher grades.
- Command words vary depending on your vocational area. So Art and Design grading grids may use different command words from Applied Science, for example.

TOP TIP

Look at this section again when you get your first assignment and check the command words against these explanations.

To obtain a pass grade

To achieve a pass you must usually demonstrate that you understand the important facts relating to a topic and can state these clearly and concisely.

Command words for a pass	Meaning
Create (or produce)	Make, invent or construct an item.
Describe	Give a clear, straightforward description that includes all the main points and links these together logically.
Define	Clearly explain what a particular term means and give an example, if appropriate, to show what you mean.
Explain … how/why	Set out in detail the meaning of something, with reasons. It is often helpful to give an example of what you mean. Start with the topic then give the 'how' or 'why'.
Identify	Distinguish and state the main features or basic facts relating to a topic.
Interpret	Define or explain the meaning of something.
Illustrate	Give examples to show what you mean.
List	Provide the information required in a list rather than in continuous writing.
Outline	Write a clear description that includes all the main points but avoid going into too much detail.
Plan (or devise)	Work out and explain how you would carry out a task or activity.
Select (and present) information	Identify relevant information to support the argument you are making and communicate this in an appropriate way.
State	Write a clear and full account.
Undertake	Carry out a specific activity.
Examples:	
Identify the main features on a digital camera.	
Outline the steps to take to carry out research for an assignment.	

To obtain a merit grade

To obtain a merit you must prove that you can apply your knowledge in a specific way.

Command words for a merit	Meaning
Analyse	Identify separate factors, say how they relate to each other and how each one relates to the topic.
Classify	Sort your information into appropriate categories before presenting or explaining it.
Compare and contrast	Identify the main factors that apply in two or more situations and explain the similarities and differences or advantages and disadvantages.
Demonstrate	Provide several relevant examples or appropriate evidence which support the arguments you are making. In some vocational areas this may also mean giving a practical performance.
Discuss	Provide a thoughtful and logical argument to support the case you are making.
Explain (in detail)	Provide details and give reasons and/or evidence to clearly support the argument you are making.
Implement	Put into practice or operation. You may also have to interpret or justify the effect or result.
Interpret	Understand and explain an effect or result.
Justify	Give appropriate reasons to support your opinion or views and show how you arrived at these conclusions.
Relate/report	Give a full account, with reasons.
Research	Carry out a full investigation.
Specify	Provide full details and descriptions of selected items or activities.
Examples: Compare and contrast the performance of two different digital cameras. Explain in detail the steps to take to research an assignment.	

To obtain a distinction grade

To obtain a distinction you must prove that you can make a reasoned judgement based on appropriate evidence.

Command words for a distinction	Meaning
Analyse	Identify the key factors, show how they are linked and explain the importance and relevance of each.
Assess	Give careful consideration to all the factors or events that apply and identify which are the most important and relevant, with reasons.
Comprehensively explain	Give a very detailed explanation that covers all the relevant points and give reasons for your views or actions.
Critically comment	Give your view after you have considered all the evidence, particularly the importance of both the relevant positive and negative aspects.
Evaluate	Review the information and then bring it together to form a conclusion. Give evidence to support each of your views or statements.
Evaluate critically	Review the information to decide the degree to which something is true, important or valuable. Then assess possible alternatives, taking into account their strengths and weaknesses if they were applied instead. Then give a precise and detailed account to explain your opinion.
Summarise	Identify/review the main, relevant factors and/or arguments so that these are explained in a clear and concise manner.
Examples:	
Assess ten features commonly found on a digital camera.	
Analyse your own ability to carry out effective research for an assignment.	

TOP TIP

Check that you understand exactly how you need to demonstrate each of the learning outcomes specified in the assignment.

Responding positively

Assignments enable you to demonstrate what you know and how you can apply it. You should respond positively to the challenge and give it your best shot. Being well organised and having confidence in your own abilities helps too, and this is covered in the next section.

Key points

- Read instructions carefully so that you don't make mistakes that can easily be avoided, such as only doing part of the set task.

- Note the assignment deadline on your planner and any interim review dates. Schedule work around these dates to make the most of reviews with your tutor.

- Check your centre's policies relating to assignments, such as how to obtain an extension or query a final grade.

- Expect command words and/or the complexity of a task to be different at higher grades, because you have to demonstrate higher-level skills.

TOP TIP

All your assignments will relate to topics you have covered and work you have done in class. They're not meant to be a test to catch you out.

Action points

1 Check your ability to differentiate between different types of command words by doing this activity.

   a) Prepare a brief description of your usual lifestyle (pass level).

   b) Describe and justify your current lifestyle (merit level).

   c) Critically evaluate your current lifestyle (distinction level).

It would be a good idea to check that your answer is accurate and appropriate by showing it to your tutor at your next tutorial.

TOP TIP

When presenting evidence for an assessment, think about the person who will be looking through it. Plan your 'pitch' well and make it easy for the assessor to match your evidence against the grading criteria.

Sample assignment

Note about assignments

All learners are different and will approach their assignment in different ways.
The sample assignment that follows shows how one learner answered a brief to achieve pass, merit and distinction level criteria. The learner work whose just one way in which grading criteria can be evidenced. There are no standard or set answers. If you produce the required evidence for each task then you will achieve the grading criteria covered by the assignment.

It is important to complete the front sheet of your assignment so that your tutor knows the work is yours and when you handed it in.

Deadlines are set to help you manage your assignments so it is very important your work is submitted on time. Check your centre's policy on this so you know what is expected.

It is worth asking your tutor to look at a draft version of your work so that you can act on their feedback and improve your work.

The evidence you will need to provide for an assignment can include, presentations, reports, discussions or practical demonstrations.

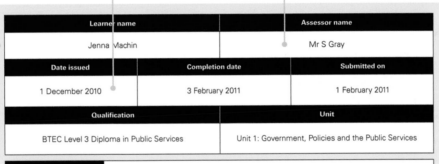

Learner name		Assessor name	
Jenna Machin		Mr S Gray	
Date issued	**Completion date**	**Submitted on**	
1 December 2010	3 February 2011	1 February 2011	
Qualification		**Unit**	
BTEC Level 3 Diploma in Public Services		Unit 1: Government, Policies and the Public Services	

Assignment title — Roles and Levels of Government

In this assignment you will have opportunities to provide evidence against the following criteria. Indicate the page numbers where the evidence can be found.

Criteria reference	To achieve the criteria the evidence must show that the learner is able to:	Task no.	Page numbers
P1	Outline the responsibilities of the levels of government in the UK	1	Pages 1–8
P2	Describe the role of government departments in relation to public services, including their responsibilities	2	Pages 1–8
M1	Explain in detail the responsibilities of the different levels of government in the UK	1	Pages 1–8
D1	Evaluate the responsibilities of the different levels of government in the UK	1	Pages 1–8

Learner declaration

I certify that the work submitted for this assignment is my own and research sources are fully acknowledged.

Learner signature: *Jenna Machin*   Date: *1 February 2011*

The criteria table is important as it shows what criteria you are aiming to achieve in your assignment.

Plagiarism is using work from another source and claiming it as your own. This is never acceptable and you must reference your work to avoid this.

Assignment brief

'Outline' means to provide a brief overview of a topic.

The scenario for your assignment will be a realistic public services situation. Scenarios help prepare you for employment and make your assignment for work focused.

Always keep the title of your assignment in mind, it will help you focus on the topic you are covering.

Unit title	Unit 1: Government, Policies and the Public Services	
Qualification	BTEC Level 3 Diploma in Public Services	
Start date	1 December 2010	
Deadline date	3 February 2011	
Assessor	Mr S Gray	

| Assignment title | Roles and Levels of Government | |

The purpose of this assignment is to:
Enable you to gain an understanding of the responsibilities of different levels of government in the UK.

Scenario
As part of a community education division of the local authority, you have been asked to present information on local, UK and European government to a group of Year 8 students as part of their PSHE lesson.

Task 1
Giving a talk to a group of Year 8 learners about the *responsibilities of the levels of government in the UK* is an interesting and exciting job because you get to interact with a range of young people and hear their views on how the country and local area is run. Your presentation should be informative and engaging and be suitable for the age of your audience.

The first thing you should do is give the learners an outline of the responsibilities of the levels of government in the UK (**P1**). Include in your brief overview the name of each level and a brief description of what each one does. This information should be displayed on your presentation slides, which the learners should be able to see and should also have a copy of. You should consider including the following levels as part of your presentation:

- European Parliament
- central government (House of Commons and House of Lords)
- devolved parliaments
- local authorities
- the monarchy
- branches of government (executive, legislative, judicial)
- the main roles at government levels, for example prime minister, government ministers, members of parliament, mayors, council members; London assembly.

To provide the learners with more information during your presentation, you should explain in detail the responsibilities of the different levels of government in the UK (**M1**). To help you remember the detail you could add some notes to your slides. The extra detail should still be about the content above but you should tell your audience about the roles and responsibilities of each level of government in more depth.

Your audience may not have heard some of the information before and they are likely to ask questions about how well each level of government performs, or they may have complaints about the levels of government from their own experience of watching the news or events in their local community. In order to address these questions you should add some additional notes to your presentation which evaluate the responsibilities of the different levels of government (**D1**) so that you have the strengths and weaknesses of each level of government close to hand if any questions do arise.

This provides evidence for P1, M1 and D1

Providing a 'detailed explanation' means examining a topic in greater depth than a simple overview.

'Evaluate' means to consider the strengths and weaknesses of a topic or idea. In this case the learner will need to examine the strengths and weaknesses of different levels of government.

'Describe' means to paint a picture with words. A description of a government department might include its structure, roles, responsibilities and key personnel.

Task 2

Key aspects of government responsibility lie with different government departments. These departments have a great deal of impact on the public services and how effective they are at their role, both nationally and in the community. So that the learners understand what these government departments do, describe the role of at least two departments in relation to the public services (**P2**). The government departments you could look at include:

- Ministry of Defence
- Home Office
- Ministry of Justice
- Department of Communities and Local Government.

You should make sure you cover the name of the department, the minister in charge and a description of the department's responsibilities so far as public services are concerned.

This provides evidence for P2

Sources of information

Textbooks

Gray, D. et al. *National Diploma in Public Services Book 1* (3rd ed) (Heinemann, 2010)

Macnaughton, N. *Edexcel Government and Politics for AS* (Heinemann, 2008)

Nugent, N. *The Government and Politics of the European Union* (6th ed) (Palgrave Macmillan, 2006)

Wright, T. *British Politics: A Very Short Introduction* (Oxford Paperbacks, 2003)

Useful websites

The European Union	**www.europa.eu**
UK Parliament	**www.parliament.uk**
The Welsh Assembly	**www.wales.gov**
The Scottish Parliament	**www.scottish.parliament.uk**
The Northern Ireland Assembly	**www.niassembly.gov.uk**

This brief has been verified as being fit for purpose			
Assessor	Mr S Gray		
Signature	*Sam Gray*	Date	*19 November 2010*
Internal verifier	Ms India Stevens		
Signature	*I Stevens*	Date	*19 November 2010*

Try to use a variety of good quality sources in your public service assignments such as books, journals, newspapers and websites. Make sure your resources are as up to date as possible.

Sample learner work

You can see the learner has provided a clear introduction showing what she will be covering in her presentation.

This slide outlines the European Parliament. This is evidence for P1. The learner also provides a detailed written explanation below which contributes to M1.

Sample learner work: page 1

Slide 1

Introduction

This presentation will cover the following levels of government and two government ministries:

- European
- Central
- Devolved Parliaments
- Local Authorities
- Main roles in government
- Ministry of Defence
- Ministry of Justice

Slide 2

European Parliament

- The European Parliament is the only directly elected body of the European Union
- It has 736 Members called MEPs
- They are elected once every five years
- Drafts EU legislation
- Controls EU budgets

The European Parliament is the only directly elected body of the European Union. It has 736 members, who are called Members of the European Parliament. These are elected from all of the member states, such as the UK, France and Germany. MEPS are voted for every five years. They are supposed to represent the citizens of the EU in the area they are elected from; so, for example, this college is the Yorkshire and Humber region and our MEP represents all the people in that area.

The Parliament drafts EU legislation. These are laws which all members of the EU must follow. Sometimes people aren't happy with EU law as they think it takes away the rights of each country to do what they want about rules on how food can be labelled, how shops should weigh items, and on really important issues to the public services such as equal opportunities, but I think it is better to have some consistency across Europe. It makes some countries behave better on issues such as human rights or the environment. For example lesbian and gay people would not be allowed in the military if the EU hadn't decided that the UK was being unlawful in banning them. The EU has a really big responsibility because its decisions affect over 400 million EU citizens. If you compare this with the UK central government, which only deals with about 60 million people, you can see how influential it really is.

The European Parliament also has joint responsibility for sorting out the budgets of the EU. Since the EU has an annual budget of around £1.5 billion, this is a really important responsibility, especially as the money comes from all the member states and they will want to make sure their money is spent sensibly.

Slides 3 and 4 clearly outline central government and the House of Commons for P1.

Sample learner work: page 2

Slide 3

Central Government

- Based in London at the Palace of Westminster
- Contains the House of Commons, the House of Lords and the Monarch
- Has responsibilities such as:
  - signing treaties or agreements with other nations
  - making laws
  - defending the nations

The Central government in the UK is based in London at the Houses of Parliament. Parliament has three parts to it: the House of Commons, the House of Lords and the Monarch. All three of these parts have to work together for decisions to be made and actions taken.

Central government has some responsibilities that no other level of government has, such as signing treaties and agreements with other nations, for example the Washington Treaty in 1949 which created NATO. Only central government has the authority to act on behalf of the whole country. If a local council signed an agreement with the French central government, then no other local authority would have to agree to it so it would be a waste of time. When central government agrees to something the whole country has to obey it, which is why this is such an important responsibility. Central governments also make laws which the whole country needs to follow. Again this makes a lot of sense because if the lower tiers of government, such as councils, made laws then every time you went from a different town or city, you might have a different set of laws. This would be really hard for people, as they might break the law without even realising it. Another important responsibility of central government is to defend us if we are under threat. Again this really couldn't be a responsibility that goes anywhere else – my local council couldn't defend me from an attack because it doesn't have any control over the armed forces. Also the situation would be ridiculous if one local council declared war on another nation but the rest of the councils didn't. Where the whole country needs to be on board with something, then it is better if central government sorts it out.

Slide 4

House of Commons

- 646 elected members of parliament called MPs
- Has responsibilities such as:
  - making laws
  - controlling finance
  - scrutinising decisions
  - creating delegated legislation
  - examining proposals from Europe
  - protecting the rights of individuals

The House of Commons. This part of Parliament contains MPs who are elected by the public to decide on how the country should be run and how our money should be raised and spent.

MPs are the ones who make laws for the country as a whole. This could be laws on criminal behaviour, how businesses should be run or human rights. They can make laws on pretty much anything if they want to. About 50% of House of Commons time is spent on making laws, so it is a really big part of their role. It is sensible that they make the bulk of the laws in the country so that we have consistency across the UK and laws apply to all of us, not just some of us. Also because the House is supposed to represent the best interests of the public, they shouldn't pass any unfair laws or laws which might hurt the public rather than protect them. This can be a bit controversial at times, as some people don't agree with laws that have been passed and accuse the government of using laws to control rather than protect.

The House of Commons has a variety of political parties within it such as Labour, Conservative and Liberal Democrats. This mix of parties is supposed to ensure that the party in power doesn't become corrupt or hurt the country, as the other parties can check up on them and ensure they are behaving lawfully. This is really important because if a government becomes corrupt they can steal money from the country for their own uses and break the human rights of the public. The other parties would not stand by and let this happen, so they act as checks and balances on the ruling party, which benefits the whole nation. The downside of this is that the House of Commons can be seen as very combative. The parties are always fighting with each other rather than working together to solve issues.

The learner has provided a detailed explanation for central government and the House of Commons for M1.

The learner has made some evaluative comments on the underpinning principles of the House of Commons, which contributes towards D1.

There is a clear outline of the House of Lords and the Monarch on slides 5 and 6. This is evidence towards P1.

Sample learner work: page 3

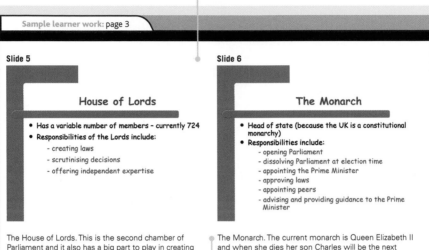

Slide 5

House of Lords

- Has a variable number of members – currently 724
- Responsibilities of the Lords include:
  - creating laws
  - scrutinising decisions
  - offering independent expertise

The House of Lords. This is the second chamber of Parliament and it also has a big part to play in creating laws. When the House of Commons has finished debating and writing laws, then they are passed to the Lords who check them and debate them as well. This means that laws are always properly scrutinised and if they are flawed the Lords will reject them and they have to go back to the Commons to be changed. This is a really good thing because without the Lords the House of Commons would have total control over law-making and would not be appropriate: there should always be someone to double check the laws.

The Lords are drawn from all parts of the UK and all walks of life, which means they often have a lot of expertise that is useful for the government.

Slide 6

The Monarch

- Head of state (because the UK is a constitutional monarchy)
- Responsibilities include:
  - opening Parliament
  - dissolving Parliament at election time
  - appointing the Prime Minister
  - approving laws
  - appointing peers
  - advising and providing guidance to the Prime Minister

The Monarch. The current monarch is Queen Elizabeth II and when she dies her son Charles will be the next monarch. In the UK the monarch is our Head of State and so has a really important role. The Queen has a power called Royal Assent, which is where she must sign and approve all laws proposed by the House of Commons and the House of Lords. The Queen also opens each session of Parliament and closes it when the country is about to have a general election. She meets with the Prime Minister regularly and gives him or her the benefit of her experience in terms of ruling the country.

When you evaluate the role of the monarch it is clear that the Queen these days has far less direct power than some of her ancestors did. She is largely a figurehead for our nation and the real power lies with the Commons and the Lords. There are some people, called republicans, who don't think we ought to have a monarch at all. They argue that in today's society you shouldn't be born into political power, but should have to earn it by being elected by the people. There are others, however, who think the Queen is actually good for our nation and helps us run our government effectively. All of the services have to swear allegiance to the Queen. I think this is wrong because really they are serving the public and their oath should be to them – but I do see both sides of the argument.

The information on the slides is explained in detail in the supporting text which contributes to M1.

The learner has evaluated the role of the Monarch and provides arguments for and against its existence. This contributes to D1.

Slides 7 and 8 clearly outline branches of government and devolved parliaments for P1.

Sample learner work: page 4

Slide 7

Branches of Government

- Three forms of power in our society – these are called branches of government
- Legislative – the power to make laws
- Executive – the power to suggest new laws and ensure existing laws are implemented
- Judicial – the power to interpret the laws and make judgements on whether laws have been broken

Branches of Government. It is really important that the branches of government are kept separate as that way no one bit of government controls the whole process – making it less likely that powers will be abused. The legislative power sits with Parliament who can make laws by following a set process. The executive power to suggest and implement laws sits with government departments and the civil service, who deal with the day-to-day running of the county. Judicial power sits with the UK courts and is implemented by judges when they make decisions in court cases.

All three branches must work together, but be independent. It would be ethically wrong if one part of government could propose, make, implement and interpret the law – peoples rights might be compromised.

Slide 8

Devolved Parliaments

- These are parliaments where power has been transferred from a central government to a regional one
  - Scottish Parliament
  - Welsh Assembly
  - Northern Ireland Assembly

The Scottish Parliament. This was created by the Scotland Act in 1998 and it deals with matters directly to do with Scotland, such as education, health, civil and criminal law. The Scottish parliament can pass its own laws, but it still must obey the laws from central government, which affect the country as a whole. The party in Scotland with the most representatives forms the government and their leader is appointed First Minister (this is like the Scottish Prime Minister) by the Queen.

The Welsh Assembly. This was created by the Government of Wales Act 1998. It is run like the Scottish Parliament and has powers over things like education, housing, planning and healthcare, but it is different from Scotland because it can't make its own civil or criminal law – it must follow central government.

The Northern Ireland Assembly. This was created by the Northern Ireland Act 1998 and it runs along the same lines as Scotland and Wales, with a First Minister and powers over education and health, etc. However the political differences in Northern Ireland, because of the long standing issues with terrorism and conflict, have meant that at times the assembly has been unstable and central government has had to step in.

Devolved parliaments can be a really good thing as they can take into account the needs of their particular area and make laws and policy which suit them better than those of central government. In theory, they should also be more in touch with the people and know what the people want. It also means that central government has less work to do and can concentrate on issues which affect all of the UK. The downside to devolved parliaments is that they can be expensive to run and some people have argued that it is a waste of money to create a devolved parliament to do what central government already does. There is also a significant problem if what a central government wants to do conflicts with what the devolved government wants.

There is clear and detailed explanatory text below each slide to contribute towards M1.

The learner has made some excellent comments about the advantages and disadvantages of devolved parliaments.

Slide 9

Local Authorities

- This is local government for towns and cities
- They have responsibilities such as:
  - registering births, deaths and marriages
  - refuse collection and disposal
  - public transport
  - street lighting
  - education
  - housing

Local Authorities. This is a really important level of government because it directly affects the area we live in and how money is spent locally. This is the part of government we see everyday because it controls traffic, public transport, education, local services and local planning. It also deals with local leisure and recreation facilities, such as pitches and sports centres. It is a necessary level of government because central government can't deal with everything that a local area needs and each area needs different things. It is therefore better to have a level of government which knows the area and the people and can make local decisions based on that.

Slide 10

Other Local Authorities

- There are lots of different forms of local government such as:
  - county councils
  - district councils
  - parish councils
  - metropolitan councils
  - unitary authorities

Slide 11 provides and overview of regional governments for P1 and follows it with a detailed explanation for M1.

The main roles at various government levels are part of the content and must be covered in the presentation if the learner is going to pass. This is covered on slides 13-18.

Sample learner work: page 6

Slide 11

Regional Governments

- There are 8 regional assemblies in England
- They have four main responsibilities:
  - regional planning
  - regional housing
  - accountability
  - advocacy and policy development

Slide 12

Main Roles at Government Levels

- Prime Minister
- Government ministers
- Members of Parliament
- Mayors
- Council members
- London Assembly

Regional Governments. These were created by the Regional Development Agencies Act 1998 and there are eight of them in England:

- East of England Regional Assembly
- North East Assembly
- South East Regional Assembly
- West Midland Regional Assembly
- East Midlands Regional Assembly
- South West Regional Assembly
- North West Regional Assembly
- Yorkshire and Humber Assembly

London has a different system, which is discussed later.

Regional assemblies are made up differently in different areas, but usually they are a mix of business people, local councillors and representatives from charities, religions and environmental groups. They get money from central and local government to spend on the region as a whole. They organise things such as transport planning, tourism to the region and housing. Many people don't know anything at all about regional government and it doesn't have a significant impact on our day-to-day lives in the way that local councils and central government do. I think this is one of the least needed levels of government.

Sample learner work: page 7

Slide 13

Prime Minister

- Leader of the political party in power
- Responsibilities include:
  - appointing and dismissing ministers and allocating their work
  - control of information
  - setting the agenda for government business
  - liaising with other world leaders

Slide 14

Government Ministers

- These are heads of government departments
- The top 20 or so make up the 'Cabinet'
- Key posts are:
  - Chancellor of the Exchequer
  - Home Secretary
  - Secretary of Defence

Slide 15

MPs

- These are elected by the public and represent areas of the country called constituencies
- MPs act on the concerns of their constituents
- They help create laws
- They vote on major political decisions

Slide 16

Mayors

- Usually appointed for one year
- They represent the council at events
- They chair meetings of the council
- They promote the area
- They support charities and community groups

Slide 17

Council Members

- Elected by the local community
- They run local councils
- They decide local taxation
- They are responsible for local:
  - transport
  - education
  - environment
  - planning

Slide 18

London Assembly

- Only has influence in London
- Investigates issues that matter to the capital
- Scrutinises the work of the Mayor of London
- Makes recommendations to the Mayor on issues and policies

Slides 21 and 23 contain additional detail on the role of the two ministries chosen. This contributes towards P2.

Slide 19 is an introduction to government departments which is the subject of P2.

The learner has chosen to describe the Ministry of Defence and the Ministry of Justice for P2.

Sample learner work: page 8

Slide 19

Role of Government Departments

- Government departments have a big role to play in the organisation and funding of the public services
- There are several department who have responsibility for the services, such as:
  - the Home Office
  - the Ministry of Defence
  - the Ministry of Justice
  - the Department of Communities and Local Government

Slide 20

The Ministry of Defence

- The current Secretary of State for Defence is Rt Hon Bob Ainsworth MP, but he is is assisted by four other ministers:
  - Bill Rammell MP – Minister of State for Armed Forces
  - Rt Hon Lord Drayson – Minister for Strategic Defence Acquisition
  - Quentin Davies MP – Minister for Defence Equipment and Support
  - Rt Hon Baroness Taylor – Minister for International Defence and Security

Slide 21

Role of the Ministry of Defence

- Responsibility for the British Army, the Royal Navy and the Royal Air Force
- The MOD decides on budgets, policy and procurement for all three armed services
- This means it has a tremendous amount of influence on the armed services
- Deciding everything from pay and conditions to equipment to locations of service

Slide 22

The Ministry of Justice

- The current Secretary of State for Justice is Jack Straw, but he is helped by five other ministers:
  - Michael Wills, Minister of State
  - Maria Eagle, Minister of State
  - Bridget Prentice, Parliamentary Under Secretary of State
  - Claire Ward, Parliamentary Under Secretary of State
  - Lord Bach, Parliamentary Under Secretary of State

Slide 23

Role of the Ministry of Justice

- This ministry has responsibility for:
  - courts
  - prisons
  - probation
- This means that it is involved in offender management from charge to release
- It decides on budgets, policy and procedures for the whole criminal justice and offender management service

Slide 24

Assignment References

- www.europa.eu
- www.parliament.uk
- Gray, D. et al. National Diploma in Public Services Book 1 (3rd ed). Heinemann, 2010
- Macnaughton, N – Edexcel Government and Politics for AS. Heinemann, 2008

The learner has listed the sources of information she has used to prepare the assignment. This shows her tutor she has researched her work and read about the topic.

Referencing is normally done to Harvard standard. Your tutor will be able to explain this to you. As a minimum a reference will contain the name of the author and the title of the work.

Observation record

Learner name	Jenna Machin
Qualification	BTEC Level 3 Diploma in Public Services
Unit number and title	Unit 1: Government, Policies and the Public Services

Description of activity undertaken (please be as specific as possible)

This was a presentation with supporting notes designed to be delivered to Year 8 learners on the roles and responsibilities of government departments and levels of government.

Grading criteria (to which the activity provides evidence)

P1: Outline the responsibilities of the levels of government in the UK.

P2: Describe the role of government departments in relation to public services, including their responsibilities.

M1: Explain in detail the responsibilities of the different levels of government in the UK.

D1: Evaluate the responsibilities of the different levels of government in the UK.

How the activity meets the requirements of the assessment and grading criteria, including how and where the activity took place

Task 1

For **P1**, The learner gave a very high quality presentation that was fit for the audience specified in the scenario. The learner's slides and verbal exposition clearly outlined the responsibilities of levels of government in the UK and covered all the associated content including European Parliament, central government (House of Commons and House of Lords), devolved parliaments, local authorities, the monarchy, branches of government (executive, legislative, judicial); and the main roles at government levels – for example prime minister, government ministers, members of parliament, mayors, council members; London Assembly. The slides were professional, notes were clear and the tone of voice and body language were good.

For **M1**, the supporting notes on the presentation were accurate and well researched and had sufficient detail. They were used to good effect in the verbal delivery of the presentation, taking the delivery of the information to a more detailed level. The learner clearly explained the responsibilities of levels of government in detail.

For **D1**, evidence for this criterion was found in the supporting notes to the presentation and in the excellent responses to questions which were asked during the presentation. The learner made clear analytical and evaluative assessments about the responsibilities of different levels of government in response to questions from the audience, which included issues such as strikes, refuse collection, perceived police harassment of young people and MP's expenses. The quality of the verbal delivery provoked some interesting and controversial discussion points from the audience. A good depth of knowledge was demonstrated and a clear ability to provide a balanced evaluation was present.

Task 2

For **P2**, the slides highlighted clearly the names of two government departments (the Ministry of Defence and the Ministry of Justice), the ministers in charge of those departments and the responsibilities that each department had to the public services. This was also very well explained to the audience in the learners' verbal delivery.

Assessor name	Mr S Gray		
Assessor signature	Sam Gray	Date	17 January 2011

Sample assessor's comments

Programme	BTEC Level 3 Diploma in Public Services	Year	2010–11
Unit number and title	Unit 1: Government, Policies and the Public Services	Learner name	Jenna Machin

Grading criteria	Achieved?
P1 Outline the responsibilities of the levels of government in the UK	Y
P2 Describe the role of government departments in relation to public services, including their responsibilities	Y
M1 Explain in detail the responsibilities of the different levels of government in the UK	Y
D1 Evaluate the responsibilities of the different levels of government in the UK	Y

Learner feedback

I liked this assignment. I'm not too good at written reports so being able to deliver a lot of the information verbally suits me a bit better. The difficulty for me was making sure I didn't put too much on my slides and using my notes to explain and evaluate the levels. This was the first time I have done a presentation this big and this detailed and I am pleased with it. I also got a lot of confidence from delivering it to an audience although I was really nervous to start with.

Assessor feedback

Jenna you did really well on this assignment. Your slides provided a clear outline of the responsibilities of different levels of government and your supporting notes and verbal delivery provided the explanation and evaluation required for the higher grades. You also covered the responsibilities of your chosen government departments to good effect. Both your slides and notes were very professional and your verbal delivery and body language were excellent. You kept the attention of your audience well and the quality of your information was well researched and accurate. This was an outstanding first piece of work and you should feel very proud of yourself. Well done!

Action plan

I would have liked to see you use some references in the notes or slides of your presentation – this is going to become really important as you complete your National Diploma. If you are uncertain how to do this come and see me and we will go through it. You could also consider using pictures, video and audio to add additional depth to your next presentation.

Assessor signature	Sam Gray	Date	10 February 2011
Learner signature	Jenna Machin	Date	15 February 2011

Step Seven: Work productively as a member of a group

Case study: Serith's Team Building Experience

'Teamwork is a really big part of the public services. All of the uniformed and non-uniformed services have to work together really closely to make society a better place and there are also lots of teams within the services who have specific jobs to do. We were learning about teamwork in class and the tutor took us outside on the football pitch to do a practical test of teamwork.

When we got there we found some blindfolds and some tents in bags. The task was to split into teams of six, put the blindfolds on and work together to put the tent up. We thought it would be really easy as our group had all been camping and we knew how to put a tent up, but it was really difficult. We couldn't seem to communicate what we needed to do and no-one was listening to anyone else. We lost bits of the tent and couldn't find them because we were blindfolded and we ended up getting quite angry with each other.

When we took the blindfolds off we saw all the groups had done really badly. Out tutor took us back into the classroom and we had to analyse what went wrong and what we could have done better. We came up with loads of solutions and the following week the tutor took us out again to see if our planning had improved our teamwork. We managed to get the tent up in a calm and organised manner – I was so pleased with our team.'

Reflection points

Have you ever been in a position where working in a team has gone wrong? What happened and what could you have done to improve the situation?

Think about why a team needs a leader. How would you choose a team leader?

In your private life, you can choose your own friends, whereas at work you are paid to work alongside many people whether you like them or not.

This applies at school or college too. Hopefully, by now, you've outgrown wanting to only work with your best friends on every project.

You may not be keen on everyone in your team, but you should still be pleasant and co-operative.

This may be harder if you are working with a partner than in a large group.

Sometimes you may be the group leader. This may inspire you, or fill you with dread. You won't be expected to develop team-leader skills overnight, but it helps if you know the basics.

First, you should understand how groups and teams work and why good teamwork is considered vital by employers.

Working in groups and teams

If you have a full- or part-time job, you already belong to a working group, or team. At school or college your class is an example of a working group.

All working groups have some common characteristics:

- doing the same type of work – though in the workplace you probably have different roles or responsibilities
- a group leader or supervisor
- a reason for working together, such as studying for the same qualification or tackling an area of work too large for someone to do it alone
- group members are dependent on each other in some way; at work you may have to cover someone's workload if they are absent.
- group members concentrate on their individual achievements and success

A team is different. As a team member you have a specific objective to achieve **together** – and this is more important than the goals of individual team members.

> **TOP TIP**
>
> Understanding how groups and teams function will help you be a better team worker and a better team leader.

These are the characteristics of a team.

- Team members have a team goal which is more important than any personal goals.
- Team members have complementary skills so that the team can achieve more than individuals working alone could achieve.
- Work is allocated to play to each person's strengths and talents.
- The team members give each other encouragement and support.
- There is collective responsibility for achieving the goal.

A good team leader acts as facilitator and motivator, and gives practical support and guidance.

Working in a team has many benefits. Team members can learn from each other and combine their skills to do a better job more quickly. Working with other people is often more enjoyable than working alone, too. Many industries rely a lot on efficient group working, from IT teams to health workers and the emergency services.

> **TOP TIP**
>
> Focusing on the task rather than on personalities is the first step in learning to work with different people, whose views may not match your own.

There are many benefits to be gained from working as a team.

Being a good team member

Everyone wants team members who are talented, positive, cheerful and full of energy. These are the key areas to focus on if you wish to be a good team member.

- **Your social skills.** This includes being courteous, treating other people as you wish to be treated, saying 'please' when you want something and thanking people who do you a favour.

- **Your temperament**. Expect people to have different views and opinions from you and don't take offence if someone disagrees with you. If you lose your temper easily, learn to walk away before you say something you may regret.

- **Your communication skills.** This includes talking and listening!

Practise saying what you mean clearly, accurately and succinctly. Be prepared to give good reasons to justify your arguments and ideas.

Allow people to finish what they're saying, without interruption, before you talk. Never shout people down. Think before you speak so that you don't upset people with tactless remarks. If you inadvertently do so, apologise.

- **Your commitment.** Always keep your promises and never let anyone down when they are depending upon you. Always do your fair share of the work, even if you don't agree with all the decisions made by your team. Tell people promptly if you are having problems so there is time to solve them. Be loyal to your team when you're talking to other people.

Being the team leader

It can be difficult to strike a balance between 'leading' the team and working with friends. You need to inspire and motivate your team without being bossy or critical.

Important points to remember about being a team leader

- Lead by example. Stay pleasant, consistent and control your temper, even under pressure.

- Everyone is different. Your ways of working may not always be the best.

- Be prepared to listen and contribute positively to a discussion.

- Encourage quieter team members to join in discussions by asking for their views.

- Be prepared to do whatever you ask other people to do.

- Note down what you say you will do, so that you don't forget.

- Discuss alternatives with people rather than giving orders.

- Be sensitive to other people's feelings. They may have personal problems or issues that affect their behaviour.

- Learn the art of persuasion.

- Act as peacemaker. Help people reach a compromise when necessary.

- Give team members the credit for their hard work or good ideas.

- Admit your mistakes. Look for a positive solution and think about what can be learned for the future, rather than making excuses.

- Praise and encourage team members who are working hard.

- Make criticisms constructively, and in private.

- Be assertive (put forward your point of view firmly) rather than aggressive (attacking other people to defend yourself.)

Some notes of caution about being a team leader

- Try to look pleasant and don't glare at people who interrupt you unexpectedly.

- Never talk about team members behind their backs.

- Don't gossip, exaggerate to make a point, spread rumours, speculate or tell lies.

- Don't expect to get your own way all the time – all good leaders back down on occasion.

- Never criticise any colleagues in front of other people. Speak to them in private and keep it constructive.

TOP TIP

Excellent ideas often come from quiet team members. Encourage everyone to make suggestions so that you don't overlook any valuable contributions.

Key points

- There are many benefits of working in a group or as a team. These include mutual support, companionship and the exchange of ideas.
- You will be expected to work co-operatively with other people at work, and during many course assignments.

- It isn't easy learning to be a team leader. Team leaders should be fair, consistent and pleasant to work with, as well as loyal and sensitive to the needs of team members.

Action points

1 Identify the role of teamwork in your area of study. Identify the team's goal and any factors you think will contribute towards its success.

2 Decide how you would handle each of the following difficult situations if you were the team leader. If you can, discuss your ideas with a friend in your class.
   a) The team needs to borrow a college video camera to record an event being held tonight. Your tutor tells you that the one you reserved last week is not working and the rest are out on loan.
   b) A member of your team has personal problems so you have given him less work to do. Now you've been accused of having favourites.
   c) A team member is constantly letting everyone down because of poor work and non-attendance at group meetings.
   d) Two team members have disagreed about how to do a task. You're not bothered how they do it as long as it gets done properly, and by the deadline.
   e) A team member becomes very aggressive whenever she is challenged in any way – no matter how mildly.

3 Identify someone who has inspired you because they've been an excellent leader. This could be someone you've met, a fictional character or a famous person. Note down what it is about them that impressed you.

TOP TIP

Team working, and bouncing ideas around, produces quicker and better results than working in isolation.

Activity: Team roles – researching Belbin

The public services work in teams throughout most of their working day, so understanding how teams work is an essential part of your National course. There are lots of theories about how people take on roles in teams. One of the most famous was developed by Dr Meredith Belbin. Briefly research Belbin's team roles and complete the table below.

- Once you have completed the table think about a group you have been in recently and consider which person in the group took which roles.
- Think particularly about the roles you did.

Role	Description	Which person?
Shaper		
Completer-Finisher		
Implementer		
Team worker		
Coordinator		
Resource Investigator		
Monitor-Evaluator		
Plant		

Step Eight: Understand how to research and analyse information

Case study: Finding and analysing information about jobs

'I'm currently doing a BTEC National Award in Public Services and one of the most difficult things I've come across is gathering information and knowing what to do with it when I've got it.

I struggle to know which bits of information are useful or relevant to my assignments and I usually end up with far too much information and then have no idea how to organise it or make sense of it.

My sister is in her third year at university, so I asked her how she manages all the information she collects for her essays and reports. She gave me her top tips for using information:

- Once you have read your assignment, plan your work into different sections such as introduction, main body and conclusion. This way you will only be researching for a small section of your assignment at a time, rather than all at once.
- Collect a wide variety of resources from books, journals, internet sources and newspapers, and then skim-read them to see how useful or relevant they are. If they contain lots of information about your topic, put them in a 'most useful' pile; if they have very little information on your topic, put them in a 'least useful' pile.

- Use highlighter pens on your research to colour code it. For example: everything that might be useful for your introduction mark in green, for your main body blue and for your conclusion pink. That way, when you come to write your work up, you know you are only looking for green information to write the introduction.

I tried the things she said, and sorting through my research and then understanding it after was much easier. I can see a real improvement in my motivation now I understand how to deal with the information I have.'

Reflection points

Do you think Daniel's sister's tips would work for you?

Why do you think you need to use a variety of different sources of information?

Is there anything that you currently do to research and analyse information that you find really useful?

How could you share your strategy with the rest of your class?

As a BTEC Level 3 National learner, you often have to find information for yourself. This skill will be invaluable in your working life, and if you continue your studies at higher education (HE) level. Sometimes the information will give you a better understanding of a topic, at other times you will research to obtain information for a project or assignment. Sometimes you may be so interested in something that you want to find out more without being told to do so!

Whatever your reason, and no matter where your information can be found, there is a good and not so good way to go about the task. This section will help if you can't find what you want, or find too much, or drift aimlessly around a library, or watch a demonstration and don't know what to ask afterwards.

Types of information

There are many types of information and many different sources. Depending on the task, these are the sources you may need to consult.

- **Verbal information.** This includes talking to friends, colleagues at work, members of your family, listening to experts explain what they do, interviewing people, talking to sales reps at an exhibition or customers about a product.

- **Printed information**. This includes information printed in newspapers, journals, magazines, books, posters, workshop manuals, leaflets and catalogues. The type of magazine or newspaper you read may have its own slant on the information, which you may have to take into account (see page 71).

- **Written information**. This includes course notes and handouts, reports and other documents in the workplace. If you want to use written information from work, you must check this is allowed, and that it doesn't contain confidential material such as financial information or staff names and addresses.

- **Graphical information.** This includes illustrations, pictures, cartoons, line drawings, graphs and photographs. Graphics can make something clearer than words alone. For example, a satnav instruction book might contain illustrations to show different procedures.

- **Electronic information.** This includes information from electronic sources such as DVDs, CD-ROMs, searchable databases, websites, podcasts, webinars (**seminars** online), emails and text messages. The huge amount of information available online is both a help and a hindrance. You can find information quickly, but the source may be unreliable, out-of-date, inaccurate or inappropriate (see page 64.)

TOP TIP

Too much information is as bad as too little, because it's overwhelming. The trick is to find good quality, relevant information and know when to call a halt to your search.

TOP TIP

Consider all appropriate sources and don't just rely on information found online.

Finding what you need

Spend a few minutes planning what to do before you start looking for information. This can save a lot of time later on.

The following steps will help you to do this.

1 Make sure you understand exactly what it is you need to know so that you don't waste time looking for the wrong thing.

2 Clarify your objectives to narrow down your search. Think about why the information is wanted and how much detail you need. For example, learners studying BTEC Nationals in Engineering and Performing Arts may both be researching 'noise' for their projects but they are likely to need different types of information and use it in different ways.

3 Identify your sources and check you know how to use them. You need to choose sources that are most likely to provide information relevant to your objectives. For example, an Engineering learner might find information on noise emissions in industry journals and by checking out specialist websites.

4 Plan and schedule your research. Theoretically, you could research information forever. Knowing when to call a halt takes skill. Write a schedule that states when you must stop looking and start sorting the information.

5 Store your information safely in a labelled folder. This folder should include printouts or photocopies of articles, notes about events you have attended or observed, photographs you've taken or sketches you've drawn. Divide your information under topic headings to make it easier to find. When you're ready to start work, re-read your assignment brief and select the items that are most closely related to the task you are doing.

TOP TIP

Allocate time for research as part of your assignment task. Take into account any interim deadlines as well as the final deadline for completing the work.

Primary and secondary research, and the law of copyright

There are two ways to research information. One is known as primary research, the other is secondary research.

Primary research

Primary research involves finding new information about an issue or topic. This might include finding out people's views about a product or interviewing an expert. When carrying out interviews, you will need to design a survey or questionnaire. Your primary research might also include observing or experiencing something for yourself, and recording your feelings and observations.

Secondary research

Secondary research involves accessing information that already exists in books, files, newspapers or on CD-ROMs, computer databases or the internet, and assessing it against your objectives.

This information has been prepared by other people and is available to anyone. You can quote from an original work provided you acknowledge the source of your information. You should put this acknowledgement in your text or in the bibliography to your text; do not claim it as your own research. You must include the author's name, year of publication, the title and publisher, or the web address if it is an online article. You should practise listing the sources of articles so

that you feel confident writing a bibliography. Use the guidance sheet issued by your centre to help you. This will illustrate the style your centre recommends.

The trick with research is to choose the best technique to achieve your objectives and this may mean using a mix of methods and resources. For example, if you have to comment on an industry event you might go to it, make notes, interview people attending, observe the event (perhaps take a video camera), and read any newspaper reports or online comments.

TOP TIP

Always make sure you make a note of where you get information from (your source). Keep it safely as it can be very difficult later on to work out where it came from!

People as a source of information

If you want to get the most out of interviewing someone, or several people, you need to prepare carefully in advance.

The following points give some general advice about getting the most out of face-to-face interviews.

- Make sure you know what questions to ask to get the information you need.
- Explain why you want the information.
- Don't expect to be told confidential or sensitive information.
- Write clear notes so that you remember who told you what, and when. (See also page 66.)
- Note the contact details of the person you are interviewing and ask whether they mind if you contact them again should you think of anything later or need to clarify your notes.
- Thank them for their help.

If you want to ask a lot of people for their opinion you may want to conduct a survey. You will need to design a questionnaire and analyse the results. This will be easier if you ask for **quantitative** responses – for example yes/no, true/false or ratings on a five-point scale – rather than opinions.

- Give careful thought to your representative sample (people whose opinions are relevant to the topic.)
- Decide how many people to survey so that the results mean something.
- Keep the survey relatively short.

- Thank people who complete it.
- Analyse the results, and write up your conclusions promptly.

TOP TIP

Test your questionnaire on volunteers before you 'go live' to check that there are no mistakes and the questions are easy to understand. Make any amendments before you conduct your 'real' survey.

Asking someone who knows a lot about a topic can be informative.

Avoiding pitfalls

Wikipedia is a good online source that covers many topics, and often in some depth. It is popular and free. However, it has an open-content policy, which means that anyone can contribute to and edit entries. People may post information, whether it is correct or not. Wikipedia is moving towards greater checks on entries, but it is still sensible to check out information you find on this site somewhere else.

Apart from inaccuracy, you may find other problems with information you obtain, especially material found online.

- **Out-of-date material.** Check the date of everything and keep only the latest version of books, newspapers or magazines. Yesterday's news may be of little use if you are researching something topical.
- **Irrelevant details.** Often, only part of an article will be relevant to your search. For example, if you are forecasting future trends in an area of work, you do not need information about its history or related problems. When learners are struggling, they sometimes 'pad out' answers with irrelevant information. If you've researched properly you can avoid this by having enough relevant information for your purposes.

- **Invalid assumptions.** This means someone has jumped to the wrong conclusion and made 2 + 2 = 5. You might do this if you see two friends chatting and think they are talking about you – whether they are or not! You can avoid problems in this area by double-checking your ideas and getting evidence to support them.

- **Bias.** This is when people hold strong views about a topic, or let their emotions or prejudices affect their judgement. An obvious example is asking a keen football fan for an objective evaluation of their team's performance!

- **Vested interests.** People may argue in a certain way because it's in their own interests to do so. For example, when the Government said Home Information Packs must be prepared for all properties being sold, the Association of Home Information Pack Providers was in favour because it trains the people who prepare the packs. The National Association of Estate Agents and Royal Institution of Chartered Surveyors were not because they thought they would lose business if people were put off selling their houses.

TOP TIP

Don't discard information that is affected by bias or vested interests. Just make it clear you know about the problem and have taken it into account.

Reading for a purpose

You may enjoy reading or you may find it tedious or difficult. If so, it helps to know there are different ways to read, depending on what you're doing. For example, you wouldn't look for a programme in a TV guide in the same way that you would check an assignment for mistakes. You can save time and find information more easily if you use the best method of reading to suit your purpose. The following are some examples of ways of reading.

- **Skim reading** is used to check new information and get a general overview.
To skim a book chapter read the first and last paragraphs, the headings, subheadings and illustrations. It also helps to read the first sentence of each paragraph.

TOP TIP

News articles are written with the key points at the beginning, so concentrate on the first paragraph or two. Feature articles have a general introduction and important information is contained in the main text.

- **Scanning** is used to see whether an article contains something you need – such as key words, dates or technical terms.
Focus on capital or initial letters for a name, and figures for a date. Technical terms may be in bold or italics.

- **Light reading** is usually done for pleasure when you are relaxed, for example, reading a magazine article. You may not remember many facts afterwards, so this sort of reading isn't suitable for learning something or assessing its value.

- **Word-by-word reading (proofreading)** is important so that you don't miss anything, such as the dosage instructions for a strong medicine. You should proofread assignments before you submit them.

- **Reading for study (active reading)** means being actively involved so that you understand the information. It is rare to be naturally good at this, so you might have to work to develop this skill.

Developing critical and analytical skills

Developing critical and analytical skills involves looking at information for any flaws in the arguments. These skills are important when you progress to work or higher education (HE), so it's useful to practise them now on your BTEC Level 3 National course.

A useful technique for understanding, analysing, evaluating and remembering what you are reading is **SQ4R**.

SQ4R is an effective method. It consists of six steps.

1 Survey first, to get a general impression. Scan the information to see what it is about, when it was written and by whom. The source, and the reason it was written, may be important. Most newspapers, for example, have their own 'slant' that affects how information is presented.

2 Question your aims for reading this material. What are you hoping to find? What questions are you expecting it to answer?

3 Read the information three or four times. The first time, aim to get a general idea of the content. Use a dictionary to look up any new words. Then read more carefully to really understand what the writer means.

4 Respond by thinking critically about the information and how it relates to the topic you are studying. Does it answer your queries partially, fully or not at all? What information is factual and what is based on opinion? Is there evidence to support these opinions? Is there a reason why the author has taken this standpoint? Do you agree with it? How does it link to other information you have read? What is the opposite argument and is there any evidence to support this? Overall, how useful is this information?

5 Record the information by noting the key points. Use this to refresh your memory, if necessary, rather than re-reading the article.

6 Review your notes against the original to check you have included all important points. If you are also preparing a presentation, reviewing your notes will help you to remember key points more easily.

TOP TIP

SQ4R is just one method of reading for study. Research others and adapt them to suit your own style.

Taking good notes

There are many occasions when you need to take notes, such as when a visiting speaker is talking to your class. There's no point taking notes unless you write them in a way that will allow you to use them later.

Note-taking is a personal activity. Some people prefer to make diagrammatical sketches with key points in boxes linked by arrows; others prefer to write a series of bullet points. You will develop your own style, but the following hints and tips might help you at the start.

- Use A4 lined paper, rather than a notebook, so that you have more space and don't need to turn over so often.
- When you're reading for study, make sure you have a dictionary, pen, notepad and highlighter to hand.
- Leave a wide margin to record your own comments or queries.
- Put a heading at the top, such as the speaker's name and topic, as well as the date.
- If you are making notes from a book or an article, remember SQ4R and read it several times first. Your notes will only be effective if you understand the information.
- Don't write in complete sentences – it takes too long.
- Leave spaces for later additions or corrections.
- Use headings to keep your notes clear and well organised.
- Only write down relevant information, including key words and phrases.

- Highlight, underline or use capitals for essential points.
- Never copy chunks of text – always use your own words.
- Clearly identify quotations, and record your sources, so that you can cite them in your work. (Note the author's name, title, publisher, date and place of publication and the page number.)

TOP TIP

Make sure your information is accurate, up-to-date, relevant and valid. Be aware of bias, and don't confuse fact with opinion.

Key points

- Useful information may be verbal, printed, written, graphical or electronic.
- Effective research means knowing exactly what you are trying to find and where to look. Know how reference media are stored in your library and how to search online. Store important information carefully.
- Primary research is original data you obtain yourself. Secondary research is information prepared by someone else. If you use this, you must quote your sources in a bibliography.
- You can search for information by skimming and scanning, and read in different ways. Reading for study means actively involving yourself with the text, questioning what you are reading and making notes to help your own understanding.
- Read widely around a topic to get different viewpoints. Don't accept everything you read as correct. Think about how it fits with other information you have obtained.
- Taking notes is a personal skill that takes time to develop. Start by using A4 lined pages with a margin, set out your notes clearly and label them. Only record essential information.

Action points

- Working with a friend, look back at the sources of information listed on page 62. For each type, identify examples of information relevant to your course that you could obtain from each source. See how many you can list under each type.
- Check your ability to find the information you need by answering each of the questions in **Activity: Finding information** on the next page. For any questions you get wrong, your first research task is to find out the correct answers as quickly as you can.
- To check your ability to skim and scan information, improve your ability to differentiate fact from opinion, summarise text and much more, go to page 94 to see how to access a useful BBC website.
- Check your ability to sort fact from opinion and spot vested interests by completing **Activity: Let's give you a tip...** on page 70. Check your ideas with the answers on page 93.

TOP TIP

Make a note of any information that you are struggling to understand so that you can discuss it with your tutor.

Activity: Finding information

Answer the following questions about finding information.

a) Four types of information that are available from the library in your centre, besides books, are:

1

2

3

4

b) When I visit the library, the way to check if a book I want is available is:

c) The difference between borrowing a book on short-term loan and on long-term loan is:

Short-term loan:

Long-term loan:

d) The journals that are stocked by the library that are relevant to my course include:

e) Useful information on the intranet at my centre includes:

f) Searchable databases and online magazines I can access include:

g) The quickest way to check if a book or journal contains the type of information I need is to:

h) The difference between a search engine, a portal, a directory site and a forum is:

i) Bookmarking useful websites means:

j) In addition to suggesting websites, Google can also provide the following types of information:

k) Specialist websites which provide useful information related to my course include:

l) Useful tips I would give to people starting on my course who need to find out information are:

Activity: Let's give you a tip...

In 2009, many businesses were struggling thanks to the credit crunch and falling consumer demand. Some, like Woolworths, closed down altogether. Others laid off staff, or announced wage cuts. Despite this, the Government approved recommendations by the Low Pay Commission to increase the minimum wage rate from October. Although the rise was only small, many unions, including Unison and Usdaw, agreed it was better than a freeze, which had been wanted by the British Chambers of Commerce and the British Retail Consortium.

The Government also announced new laws to stop restaurants and bars using tips to top up staff pay to the minimum level. *The Independent* newspaper claimed its 'fair tips, fair pay' campaign had won the day. It also reported that the British Hospitality Association was claiming this could result in up to 45,000 job losses. The Unite union also carried out a campaign and its General Secretary claimed the decision a triumph for the poorly paid. Not everyone agreed. Some thought there should be no tipping at all, as in Australia. Others said the Canadian system was best – wages are low but generous tips are left, and this motivates staff to give excellent service.

a) Look at the table below. In your view, which of the statements are facts and which are opinions? In each case, justify your view.

Statement	Fact or opinion?	Justification
i) Having a national minimum wage helps low-paid workers.		
ii) Over one million people will benefit from the minimum wage increase.		
iii) The new law on tips will stop restaurants paying below minimum wage rates.		
iv) Using the Australian system of no tips would be better.		
v) The Canadian system guarantees good service.		
vi) 45,000 job losses will occur in the hospitality industry.		

b) All newspapers have their own way of putting forward the news. Go to page 94 to see how you can access a website which will help you to compare the way that news is reported in different newspapers.

Compare six different newspapers and make notes on:

i) the type of stories covered

ii) the way views are put forward.

Activity: How to go about your research

Your tutor has asked you to research a variety of public services and compare their terms and conditions, such as pay, retirement, training, etc. This is a big task and will require a lot of information gathering and then a lot of time spent comparing what you find. Consider the questions below:

1 Where could you locate the information you require? List as many different resources as you can:

2 How could you sort out the resources to make sure you are using the best possible sources of information?

3 What techniques could you use to extract the relevant information from all the different resources you have gathered?

4 What would be a suitable way or presenting all the comparisons so your tutor knows you have done enough research and you have analysed what you have found?

Step Nine: Make an effective presentation

Case study: Well prepared presentations

Learners at Farpoint Academy have been undertaking additional classes to prepare them for assessed presentations. The classes are run by one of the public service tutors. He noticed three years ago that presentations were an area which made learners feel very nervous and uncomfortable because they were unused to any kind of presentation, particularly in front of an audience. The public services often have to do presentations as part of their working day, such as fire safety presentations in schools, army presentations in colleges and property safety protection in the community. Learning how to give a professional presentation will be an advantage, regardless of which service you join.

Each public service year group since that time has been given the opportunity to learn how presentations are done and practice some in front of the rest of the group before having to deliver assessed presentations in their public services units.

They are taught skills such as researching, preparing and presenting which ranges from which information sources to use to what to wear on the day. The learners are now more confident in their presentation abilities and the average grades on presentation-based assignments are higher.

Reflection points

Do you think you are the kind of person who gets nervous about presentations? If so why?

How do you think extra preparation sessions would help you develop your skills further?

If your school or college doesn't offer extra sessions, what can you do to improve on your own?

Making a presentation can be nerve-wracking. It involves several skills, including planning, preparation and communication. It tests your ability to work in a team, speak in public and use IT (normally PowerPoint.) You also have to stay calm under pressure. However, as it is excellent practice for your future, you can expect presentations to be a common method of assessing your performance.

TOP TIP

When giving a presentation, keep to time, get to the point and use your time well.

Good planning and preparation

Being well prepared, and rehearsing beforehand, helps your confidence and your presentation. The following points will help you to do this.

- If you're part of a team, find out everyone's strengths and weaknesses and divide work fairly taking these into account. Decide how long each person should speak, who should introduce the team and who will summarise at the end.

- Take into account your time-scale, resources and team skills. A simple, clear presentation is better – and safer – than a complicated one.

- If you're using PowerPoint, make slides more interesting by avoiding a series of bulleted lists and including artwork. Print PowerPoint notes for the audience. Use a fuller set of notes for yourself, as a prompt.

- Check the venue and time.

- Decide what to wear and check it's clean and presentable.

- Prepare, check and print your handouts.

- Decide, as a team, the order in which people will speak, bearing in mind the topic.

- Discuss possible questions and how to answer them.

- Rehearse beforehand to check your timings.

If you prepare properly you can really enjoy giving a presentation.

TOP TIP

Rehearsing properly allows you to speak fluently, just glancing at your notes to remind you of the next key point.

On the day, you can achieve a better performance if you:

- arrive in plenty of time
- calm your nerves by taking deep breaths before going in front of your audience
- introduce yourself clearly, and smile at the audience
- avoid reading from your screen or your notes
- explain what you are going to do – especially if giving a demonstration – do it and then review what you've done
- say you will deal with questions at the end of any demonstration
- answer questions honestly – don't exaggerate, guess or waffle
- respond positively to all feedback, which should be used to improve your performance next time.

TOP TIPS

Make sure you can be heard clearly by lifting your head and speaking a little more slowly and loudly than normal.

Key points

- When making a presentation, prepare well, don't be too ambitious and have several rehearsals.
- When giving a demonstration, explain first what you are going to do and that you will answer questions at the end.

Case study: Learner quotes about making presentations

Most people start off feeling uncomfortable about talking in front of a group of people, whether you know them or not. This is what some real learners have said about having to give presentations as part of their BTEC course.

'I actually feel more comfortable giving a presentation rather than having to write an essay. What I really enjoy about it is the fact that sometimes we have to prepare a presentation as a whole group. I like that we work together to find information and then we take turns presenting different points. The fact that I am not the only one out there and I am part of a supportive team makes it fun for me.'
Gabriela, 16, BTEC Level 2 First in Performing Arts

'Although presentations are very stressful, when I present my work it helps to hang my ideas together and I find I can express what I want to say more clearly than when I write things down. Instant feedback is helpful and boosts my confidence for the next time.'
Ethan, 19, BTEC Level 2 First in Creative Media Production

'I think presentations are useful but I find them difficult to deliver – relying heavily on my memory, which is very nerve-wracking. We were told that presentation would be part of our assessment. I really worried about it and couldn't sleep the night before – stressing out about what I was going to say. I hated the first few minutes, but after that I was OK.'
Will, 16, BTEC Level 2 First in Engineering

'I was very nervous about presenting to my class until I took part in the Young Enterprise scheme and had to present the results of our project to over 200 people including the mayor! After that, presenting to my class mates didn't feel too nerve wracking at all.'
Lizzy, 17, BTEC Level 2 First in Business

'I used to dread presentations on my course, but found that if I went through my notes again and again until I knew the presentation inside out, it made it much easier and the presentations generally went well.'
Javinder, 17, BTEC Level 3 National in Construction

Activity: All right on the night?

Read the following account and answer the questions that follow. If possible, compare ideas with a friend in your class.

Gemma looked around in exasperation. The team were on the final rehearsal of their presentation and nothing was going right. Amaya seemed to think it was funny. 'Honestly, Gemma, why don't you just chill for a bit?' she suggested. 'You know what they say – a bad dress rehearsal means we'll do really well tomorrow!'

Gemma glared at her. 'Well, can I make a suggestion, too, Amaya,' she retorted. 'Why don't you just concentrate for a change? Sprawling around and dissolving into giggles every five minutes isn't helping either.'

She turned to Adam. 'And I thought you were going to build a simple model,' she said, 'not one that falls apart every time you touch it.'

Adam looked crest-fallen. 'But I wanted to show how it worked.'

'How it's supposed to work, you mean!' raged Gemma, all her worries and anxieties now coming to the fore. 'We'll look stupid if it ends up in bits on the floor tomorrow and Amaya just falls about laughing again.'

'And Imran,' continued Gemma, turning her sights on the last member of the team, 'why is it so difficult for you to count to three minutes? We've agreed over and over again we'll each talk for three minutes and every time you get carried away with the sound of your own voice and talk for twice as long. It just means we're going to overrun and get penalised. And stop trying to wriggle out of answering questions properly. For heaven's sake, if you don't know the answer, how hard is it just to say so?'

Silence fell. No-one looked at each other. Adam fiddled with his model and something else fell off. Amaya wanted to laugh but didn't dare.

Imran was sulking and vowed never to say anything ever again. 'You wait,' he thought. 'Tomorrow I'll race through my part in one minute flat. And then what are you going to do?'

1 Identify the strengths and weaknesses of each member of the presentation team.

Name	Strengths	Weaknesses
Gemma		
Amaya		
Adam		
Imran		

2 What have the team done right, so far, in getting ready for their presentation?

3 Why do you think they are having problems?

4 If you were Gemma's tutor, what advice would you give her at this point?

Activity: Presentation checklist

A good presentation is made up of several key aspects:

- Preparation
- Delivery
- Appearance
- Research
- Visual Aids.

Consider a presentation you have done or are currently preparing for your BTEC National in Public Services. Use the checklist below to see if your presentation will be as professional as you can make it.

TOP TIPS

When making a PowerPoint presentation, don't just read out what it says on the slides. The audience can do this. Use the slides as prompt cards.

Research	
Have you used a variety of sources?	
Have you recorded your sources in a reference list or bibliography?	
Does everything you have included relate directly to the question?	
Is your research good quality and appropriate at National level?	
Presentation	
Have you introduced yourself and told the audience the title of the presentation?	
Does your introduction grab the audience's attention and explain your objectives?	
Are these main points in logical sequence?	
Are you main points backed up my evidence or references from your research?	
Does your presentation flow well?	
Do the main points need support from visual aids, such as diagrams or pictures?	
Is the conclusion strong?	
Have you tied your conclusions back to the introduction?	
Delivery	
Do you really know your topic? You are likely to be asked questions.	
Do you have supporting notes to help you?	
Have you checked where you will be doing your presentation? Is it suitable?	
Have you produced a handout or copy of your slides for your audience and tutor?	
Have you checked your visual aids to ensure they are working and you know how to use them?	
Appearance	
Are you dressed appropriately for your audience?	
Have btyou practiced resour speech and body language?	
Can you maintain eye contact with your audience?	
Visual Aids	
Are your visual aids easy to read and understand?	
Have you checked them for spelling and grammar errors?	

Step Ten: Maximise your opportunities and manage your problems

Case study: Making the most of opportunities and dealing with problems

Jenna's experience

'I had only been at college a few weeks when my dad lost his job. He is a steelworker and lots of the factories are closing at the moment because of the recession. It's just me and my dad at home and he was gutted about his job, especially because it looked like he would have to retrain to get another job.

It was really hard seeing him stay at home all day; he has always worked and likes to be busy. It was starting to affect me too because the house always felt depressing and we didn't have any money.

I think some people in that situation might just get resentful and angry but I have never thought that it is my dad's job to take care of everything; we work as a team. I've been brought up to be independent and as soon as I got over the shock of it all I started to think about what I could do to help.

I've had a Saturday job for a couple of years, but it doesn't really bring much money in, certainly not enough to help out the family and Dad was dead against me working too many hours in case it affected my studies.

One day at college we had a visiting speaker from the local Territorial Army regiment. It seemed like a perfect solution and a great opportunity. I could join the TA, earn some money to help the family out, and get some great training which will help me on my public services course and in the future.

That was three months ago now and I'm really enjoying my time at the TA. It has really enhanced my performance on my public service course and the money is really helping out while Dad retrains.'

Reflection points

What do you think you would have done in Jenna's situation?

Have you ever faced problems like Jenna?

How did you deal with them?

If your course takes one or two years to complete, then it is highly likely that you will experience some highs and lows in that time. You may find one or two topics harder than the rest. There may be distractions in your personal life to cope with. All of which means than you may not always be able to do your best.

It is, therefore, sensible to have an action plan to help you cope. It's also wise to plan how to make the best of opportunities for additional experiences or learning. This section shows you how to do this.

TOP TIP

Because life rarely runs smoothly, it's sensible to capitalise on the opportunities that come your way and have a plan to deal with problems.

Making the most of your opportunities

There will be many opportunities for learning on your course, not all of which will be in school or college. You should prepare for some of the following to maximise the opportunities that each offer.

- **External visits**. Prepare in advance by reading about relevant topics. Make notes when you are there. Write up your notes neatly and file them safely for future reference.

- **Visiting speakers**. Questions can usually be submitted to the speaker in advance. Think carefully about information that you would find helpful. Make notes, unless someone has been appointed to make notes for the whole group. You may be asked to thank the speaker on behalf of your group.

- **Work experience**. If work experience is an essential part of your course, your tutor will help you to organise your placement and tell you about the evidence you need to obtain. You may also get a special logbook in which to record your experiences. Read and re-read the units to which your evidence will apply and make sure you understand the grading criteria and what you need to obtain. Make time to write up your notes, logbook and/or diary every night (if possible), while everything is fresh in your mind.

- **In your own workplace**. If you have a full-time or part-time job, watch for opportunities to find out more about relevant topics that relate to your course, such as health and safety, teamwork, dealing with customers, IT security and communications. Your employer will have had to address all of these issues. Finding out more about these issues will broaden your knowledge and give more depth to your assessment responses.

- **Television, newspapers, podcasts and other information sources**. The media can be an invaluable source of information. Look out for news bulletins relating to your studies, as well as information in topical television programmes – from *The Apprentice* to *Top Gear*. You can also read news headlines online. Podcasts are useful, too. It will help if you know what topics you will be studying in the months to come, so you can spot useful opportunities as they arise.

TOP TIP

Remember that you can use online catch-up services, such as the BBC iPlayer or 4oD (for Channel 4 shows) to see TV programmes you have missed recently.

Minimising problems

Hopefully, any problems you experience during your course will only be minor; such as struggling to find an acceptable working method with someone in your team.

You should already know who to talk to about these issues, and who to go to if that person is absent or you would prefer to talk to someone else. If your problems are affecting your work, it's sensible to see your tutor promptly. It is a rare learner who is enthusiastic about every topic and gets on well with everyone else doing the course, so your tutor won't be surprised and will give you useful guidance (in confidence) to help.

TOP TIP

Don't delay talking to someone in confidence if you have a serious problem. If your course tutor is unavailable, talk to another staff member you like and trust.

Other sources of help

If you are unfortunate enough to have a more serious personal problem, the following sources of help may be available in your centre.

- **Professional counselling.** There may be a professional counselling service. If you see a counsellor, nothing you say during the session can be mentioned to another member of staff without your permission.

- **Complaint procedures.** If you have a serious complaint, the first step is to talk to your tutor. If you can't resolve your problem informally, there will be a formal learner complaint procedure. These procedures are used only for serious issues, not for minor difficulties.

- **Appeals procedures.** If you disagree with your final grade for an assignment, check the grading criteria and ask the subject tutor to explain how the grade was awarded. If you are still unhappy, talk to your personal tutor. If you still disagree, you have the right to make a formal appeal.

- **Disciplinary procedures.** These exist for when learners consistently flout a centre's rules and ensure that all learners are dealt with in the same way. Hopefully, you will never get into trouble, but you should make sure that you read these procedures carefully to see what could happen if you did. Remember that being honest and making a swift apology is always the wisest course of action.

- **Serious illness.** Whether this involves you, a family member or a close friend, it could affect your attendance. Discuss the problem with your tutor promptly; you will be missing information from the first day you are absent. There are many solutions in this type of situation – such as sending notes by post and updating you electronically (providing you are well enough to cope with the work.)

TOP TIP

It's important to know your centre's procedures for dealing with important issues such as complaints, major illnesses, learner appeals and disciplinary matters.

Key points

- Don't miss opportunities to learn more about relevant topics through external visits, listening to visiting speakers, work experience, being at work or even watching television.

- If you have difficulties or concerns, talk to your tutor, or another appropriate person, promptly to make sure your work isn't affected.

Action points

1 Prepare in advance to maximise your opportunities.
  a) List the opportunities available on your course for obtaining more information and talking to experts. You can check with your tutor to make sure you've identified them all.
  b) Check the content of each unit you will be studying so that you know the main topics and focus of each.
  c) Identify the information that may be relevant to your course on television, on radio, in newspapers and in podcasts.

2 Make sure you know how to cope if you have a serious problem.
  a) Check your centre's procedures so you know who to talk to in a crisis, and who to contact if that person is absent.
  b) Find out where you can get hold of a copy of the main procedures in your centre that might affect you if you have a serious problem. Then read them.

Activity: Dealing with problems

Hopefully you will not encounter any major problems while on your BTEC National in Public Services. However, sometimes problems are unavoidable. What problems might you encounter and what can you do about them?

Problem	Solution

AND FINALLY ...

Refer to this Study Skills Guide whenever you need to remind yourself about something related to your course. Keep it in a safe place so that you can use it whenever you need to refresh your memory. That way, you'll get the very best out of your course – and yourself!

Your Study Skills Guide will help you gain the skills you need for success.

Skills building

This section has been written to help you improve the skills needed to do your best in your assignments. You may be excellent at some skills already, others may need further work. The skills you can expect to demonstrate on your course include:

- your personal, learning and thinking skills (**PLTS**)
- your **functional skills** of ICT, maths/numeracy and English
- your proofreading and document production skills.

Personal, learning and thinking skills (PLTS)

These are the skills, personal qualities and behaviour that enable you to operate more independently, work more confidently with other people and be more effective at work. You'll develop these on your BTEC Level 3 National course through a variety of experiences and as you take on different roles and responsibilities.

The skills are divided into six groups:

1 **Independent enquirers** can process and evaluate information they investigate from different perspectives. They can plan what to do and how to do it, and take into account the consequences of making different decisions.

2 **Creative thinkers** generate and explore different ideas. They make connections between ideas, events and experiences that enable them to be inventive and imaginative.

3 **Reflective learners** can assess themselves and other people. They can evaluate their own strengths and limitations. They set themselves realistic goals, monitor their own performance and welcome feedback.

4 **Team workers** collaborate with other people to achieve common goals. They are fair and considerate to others, whether as a team leader or team member, and take account of different opinions.

5 **Self-managers** are well-organised and show personal responsibility, initiative, creativity and enterprise. They look for new challenges and responsibilities and are flexible when priorities change.

6 **Effective participators** play a full part in the life of their school, college, workplace or wider community by taking responsible action to bring improvements for others as well as themselves.

Action points

1 Many parts of this Study Skills Guide relate to the development of your own personal, learning and thinking skills. For each of the following, suggest the main skill groups to which the chapter relates. Refer to the box above and write a number next to each chapter title below.

a) Use your time wisely. ____

b) Understand how to research and analyse information. ____

c) Work productively as a member of a group. ____

d) Understand yourself. ____

e) Utilise all your resources. ____

f) Maximise your opportunities and manage your problems. ____

2 You have been on your BTEC National course for a few months now and, although everyone is enjoying the work, you realise that some of the learners have complaints.

Firstly, several learners object to an increase in the price of printouts and photocopying, on the basis that they can't do good work for their assignments if this is too expensive. You disagree and think that the prices are reasonable, given the cost of paper.

Secondly, a timetable change means your 2 pm – 4 pm Friday afternoon class has been moved to 9 am – 11 am. Some learners are annoyed and want it changed back, while others are delighted.

a) For the first problem, identify four factors which could indicate that those complaining about the price rise might be justified.

1

2

3

4

b) For the second problem:

  i) Think about which learners in your group would be most affected by the timetable change. Who might be most disturbed? Who might benefit from the earlier start?

  ii) Try to think of a creative solution, or compromise, that would please both groups.

c) During the discussions about these issues, some quieter members of the class are often shouted down by the more excitable members. Suggest a strategy for dealing with this, which everyone is likely to accept.

You can also check your ideas with the suggestions given on page 93.

3 a) Complete the chart opposite, identifying occasions when you may need to demonstrate personal, learning and thinking skills in your future career. Alternatively, apply each area to a part-time job you are currently doing.

b) Identify areas where you think you are quite strong and put a tick in the 'S' column. Check that you could provide evidence to support this judgement, such as a time when you have demonstrated this skill.

c) Now consider areas where you are not so good and put a cross in the 'W' column.

d) Then practise self-management by identifying two appropriate goals to achieve over the next month and make a note of them in the space provided. If possible, talk through your ideas at your next individual tutorial.

Personal, learning and thinking skills for future career/current part-time job				
Skill group	**Example skills**	**Occasions when you use/ will use skill**	**S**	**W**
Independent enquirers	Finding information Solving problems Making decisions Reconciling conflicting information or views Justifying decisions			
Creative thinkers	Finding imaginative solutions Making original connections Finding new ways to do something Opportunities for being innovative and inventive			
Reflective learners	Goals you may set yourself Reviewing your own progress Encouraging feedback Dealing with setbacks or criticism			
Team workers	Working with others Coping with different views to your own Adapting your behaviour Being fair and considerate			
Self-managers	Being self-starting and showing initiative Dealing positively with changing priorities Organising your own time and resources Dealing with pressure Managing your emotions			
Effective participators	Identifying issues of concern to others Proposing ways forward Identifying improvements for others Influencing other people Putting forward a persuasive argument			
Goals	1			
	2			

Functional skills

Functional skills are practical skills that everyone needs to have in order to study and work effectively. They involve using and applying English, maths and ICT.

Improving your literacy skills

Your written English communication skills

A good vocabulary increases your ability to explain yourself clearly. Work that is presented without spelling and punctuation errors looks professional, and increases the likelihood of someone understanding your intended meaning. Your written communication skills will be tested in many assignments. You should work at improving areas of weakness, such as spelling, punctuation or vocabulary.

Try the following to help you improve your written communication skills:

- Read more as this introduces you to new words, and it will help your spelling.
- Look up new words in a dictionary and try to use them in conversation.
- Use a Thesaurus (you can access one electronically in Word) to find alternatives to words you use a lot, this adds variety to your work.
- Never use words you don't understand in the hope that they sound impressive.
- Write neatly, so people can read what you've written.
- Do crosswords to improve your word power and spelling.
- Improve your punctuation – especially the use of apostrophes – either by using an online programme or by using a communication textbook.
- Go to page 94 to see how to gain access to some helpful websites.

Verbal and non-verbal communication (NVC) skills

Talking appropriately means using the right words and 'tone'; using the right body language means sending positive signals to reinforce this message – such as smiling at someone when you say 'Hello'. Both verbal and non-verbal communication skills are essential when dealing with people at work.

The following are some hints for successful communication:

- Be polite, tactful and sensitive to other people's feelings.
- Think about the words and phrases that you like to hear, and use them when communicating with other people.
- Use simple language so that people can understand you easily. Explain what you mean, when necessary.
- Speak at the right pace. Don't speak so slowly that everyone loses interest, or so fast that no-one can understand you.
- Speak loudly enough for people to hear you clearly – but don't shout!
- Think about the specific needs of different people – whether you are talking to a senior manager, an important client, a shy colleague or an angry customer.
- Recognise the importance of non-verbal communication (NVC) so that you send positive signals by smiling, making eye contact, giving an encouraging nod or leaning forwards to show interest.
- Read other people's body language to spot if they are anxious or impatient so that you can react appropriately.

TOP TIP

Make sure you use the right tone for the person you're talking to. Would you talk to an adult in the same way you'd talk to a very young child?

Action points

1 Go to page 94 to see how to gain access to websites which can help you to improve your literacy skills.

2 A battery made in China contained the following information.

> **DO NOT CONNECT IMPROPERLY**
>
> **CHARGE OR DISPOSE OF IN FIRE**

a) Can you see any problems with this? Give a reason for your answer.

b) Reword the information so that it is unambiguous.

3 If you ever thought you could completely trust the spellchecker on your computer, type the text given in box A on the next page into your computer. Your spellchecker will not highlight a single error; yet even at a glance you should be able to spot dozens of errors!

Read the passage in box A and try to understand it. Then rewrite it in box B on the next page without spelling, grammatical or punctuation errors. Compare your finished work with the suggested version on page 93.

Box A

Anyone desirable to write books or reports, be they short or long, should strive too maximise they're optimal use of one's English grammar and obliviously there is an need for correct spelling two one should not neglect punctuation neither.

Frequent lea, many people and individuals become confusing or just do not no it, when righting, when words that mean different, when sounding identically, or when pronounced very similar, are knot too bee spelled inn the same whey. The quay two suck seeding is dew care, a lack off witch Leeds too Miss Spellings that mite otherwise of bean a voided. Spell chequers donut find awl missed takes.

Despite all the pitfalls how ever, with practise, patients and the right altitude, any one can soon become a grate writer and speaker, as what I did.

Box B Now rewrite the passage in the space below without errors.

4 In each of the statements listed in the table below, suggest what the body language described might mean.

Statement	What might this body language mean?
a) You are talking to your manager when he steps away from you and crosses his arms over his chest.	
b) You are talking to your friend about what she did at the weekend but she's avoiding making eye contact with you.	
c) During a tutorial session, your tutor is constantly tapping his fingers on the arm of his chair.	
d) Whenever you talk to your friend about your next assignment she bites her lower lip.	

Improving your maths or numeracy skills

If you think numeracy isn't relevant to you, then think again! Numeracy is an essential life skill. If you can't carry out basic calculations accurately then you will have problems, perhaps when you least expect them. You'll often encounter numbers in various contexts – sometimes they will be correctly given, sometimes not. Unless you have a basic understanding about numeracy, you won't be able to tell the difference.

Good numeracy skills will improve your ability to express yourself, especially in assignments and at work. If you have problems, there are strategies that you can practise to help:

- Do basic calculations in your head, then check them on a calculator.
- Ask your tutor for help if important calculations give you problems.
- When you are using your computer, use the onscreen calculator (or a spreadsheet package) to do calculations.
- Investigate puzzle sites and brain training software, such as Dr Kageyama's Maths Training by Nintendo.

Action points

1 To gain access to websites which can help you to improve your numeracy skills, see the Accessing website links section on page 94.

2 Try the following task with a friend or family member.

Each of you should write down 36 simple calculations in a list, e.g. 8 × 6, 19 − 8, 14 + 6. Exchange lists. See who can answer the most calculations correctly in the shortest time.

3 Figures aren't always what they appear to be. For example, Sophie watches *Who Wants To Be A Millionaire?* She hears Chris Tarrant say that there have been over 500 shows, with 1200 contestants who have each won over £50,000 on average. Five people have won £1 million.

Sophie says she is going to enter because she is almost certain to win more than £50,000 and could even win a million pounds.

a) On the figures given, what is the approximate total of money won over 500 shows (to the nearest £ million)?

b) Assuming that Sophie is chosen to appear on the show, and makes it on air as a contestant, do you think Sophie's argument that she will 'almost certainly' win more than £50,000 is correct? Give a reason for your answer. (The correct answer is on page 94.)

4 You have a part-time job and have been asked to carry out a survey on the usage of the drinks vending machine. Of the 500 people surveyed:
- 225 use the machine to buy one cup of coffee only
- 100 use the machine to buy one cup of tea only
- 75 use the machine to buy one cup of cold drinks only
- 50 use the machine to buy one cup of hot chocolate only
- the rest are non-users
- the ratio of male to female users is 2:1.

a) How many men in your survey use the machine?

b) How many women in your survey use the machine?

c) Calculate the proportion of the people in your survey that use the machine. Express this as a fraction and a percentage.

d) What is the ratio of coffee drinkers to tea drinkers in your survey?

e) What is the ratio of coffee drinkers to hot chocolate drinkers in your survey?

f) If people continue to purchase from the machine in the same ratio found in your survey, and last month 1800 cups of coffee were sold, what would you expect the sales of the cold drinks to be?

g) Using the answer to f), if coffee costs 65p and all cold drinks cost 60p, how much would have been spent in total last month on these two items?

Improving your ICT skills

Good ICT skills are an asset in many aspects of your daily life and not just for those studying to be IT practitioners.

The following are ways in which you can Improve your ICT skills:

- Check that you can use the main features of the software packages you need to produce your assignments, eg Word, Excel and PowerPoint.
- Choose a good search engine and learn to use it properly. Go to page 94 to see how to access a useful website.
- Developing and using your IT skills enables you to enhance your assignments. This may include learning how to import and export text and artwork from one package to another; taking digital photographs and inserting them into your work and/or creating drawings or diagrams by using appropriate software.

Action points

1 Check your basic knowledge of IT terminology by identifying each of these items on your computer screen:

a) taskbar	**f)** scroll bars
b) toolbar	**g)** status bar
c) title bar	**h)** insertion point
d) menu bar	**i)** maximise/ minimise button.
e) mouse pointer	

2 Assess your IT skills by identifying the packages and operations you find easy to use and those that you find more difficult. If you use Microsoft Office products (Word, PowerPoint, Access or Excel) you can find out more about improving your skills online. Go to page 94 to see how to access a useful website.

3 Search the internet to find a useful dictionary of IT terms. Bookmark it for future use. Find out the meaning of any of the following terms that you don't know already:

a) portal

b) cached link

c) home page

d) browser

e) firewall

f) HTML

g) URL

h) cookie

i) hyperlink

j) freeware.

Proofreading and document preparation skills

Improving your keyboard, document production and general IT skills can save you hours of time. When you have good skills, the work you produce will be of a far more professional standard.

- Think about learning to touch type. Your centre may have a workshop you can join, or you can use an online program – go to page 94 to see how to access a useful website.

- Obtain correct examples of any document formats you will have to use, such as a report or summary, either from your tutor, the internet or from a textbook.

- Proofread all your work carefully. A spellchecker won't find all your mistakes, so you must read through it yourself as well.

- Make sure your work looks professional by using a suitable typeface and font size, as well as reasonable margins.

- Print your work and store the printouts neatly, so that it stays in perfect condition for when you hand it in.

Action points

1 You can check and improve your typing skills using online typing sites – see link in previous section.

2 Check your ability to create documents by scoring yourself out of 5 for each of the following questions, where 5 is something you can do easily and 0 is something you can't do at all. Then focus on improving every score where you rated yourself 3 or less.

I know how to:

a) create a new document and open a saved document _____

b) use the mouse to click, double-click and drag objects _____

c) use drop-down menus _____

d) customise my toolbars by adding or deleting options _____

e) save and/or print a document _____

f) create folders and sub-folders to organise my work _____

g) move a folder I use regularly to My Places _____

h) amend text in a document _____

i) select, copy, paste and delete information in a document _____

j) quickly find and replace text in a document _____

k) insert special characters _____

l) create a table or insert a diagram in a document _____

m) change the text size, font and colour _____

n) add bold, italics or underscore _____

o) create a bullet or numbered list _____

p) align text left, right or centred _____

q) format pages before they are printed _____

r) proofread a document so that there are no mistakes _____.

Answers

Activity: Let's give you a tip... (page 70)

a) i) Fact

ii) Opinion – the number cannot be validated

iii) Fact

iv) Opinion

v) Opinion

vi) Opinion – again the number is estimated

Skills building answers

PLTS Action points (page 83)

1 a) Use your time wisely = **5** Self-managers

b) Understand how to research and analyse information = **1** Independent enquirers, **5** Self-managers

c) Work productively as a member of a group = **4** Team workers, **6** Effective participators

d) Understand yourself = **3** Reflective learners

e) Utilise all your resources = **5** Self-managers

f) Maximise your opportunities and manage your problems = **1** Independent enquirers, **2** Creative thinkers, **3** Reflective learners, **5** Self-managers

2 a) Factors to consider in relation to the increased photocopying/printing charges include: the comparative prices charged by other schools/colleges, how often there is a price rise, whether any printing or photocopying at all can be done without charge, whether there are any concessions for special tasks or assignments, the availability of class sets of books/popular library books for loan (which reduces the need for photocopying.)

b) i) An earlier start will be more likely to negatively affect those who live further away and who are reliant on public transport, particularly in rural areas. The earlier finish will benefit anyone who has a part-time job that starts on a Friday afternoon or who has after college commitments, such as looking after younger sisters or brothers.

ii) The scope for compromise would depend on whether there are any classes between 11 am and 2 pm on a Friday, whether tutors had any flexibility and whether the new 9 am – 11 am class could be moved to another time or day.

c) One strategy would be to allow discussion for a set time, ensure everyone had spoken, then put the issue to a vote. The leader should prompt suggestions from quieter members by asking people individually what they think.

Literacy skills action points (page 87)

2 a) The statement reads as if it is acceptable to either charge it or dispose of it in fire.

b) Do not connect this battery improperly. Do not recharge it and do not dispose of it in fire.

3 Anyone who wishes to write books or reports, whether short or long, should try to use English grammatically. Obviously there is a need for correct spelling, too. Punctuation should also not be neglected.

Frequently, people confuse words with different meanings when they are writing, especially when these sound identical or very similar, even when they must not be spelled in the same way. The key to succeeding is due care, a lack of which leads to misspellings that might otherwise have been avoided. Spellcheckers do not find all mistakes.

Despite all the pitfalls, however, with practice, patience and the right attitude, anyone can soon become a great writer and speaker, like me.

4 Possible answers

a) Stepping backwards and crossing arms across the chest might indicate that your manager is creating a barrier between you and himself, or that he is angry.

b) Your friend might be feeling guilty about what she did at the weekend or not confident that you will approve of what she tells you.

c) Your tutor might be frustrated as he has many things to do and so wants the tutorial to be over quickly.

d) Your friend might be anxious about the next assignment or about the time she has to complete it.

Numeracy action points (page 90)

3 a) £60 million

b) Sophie's argument is incorrect as £50,000 is an average, i.e. some contestants will win more, but many will win much less. The distribution of prizes is greater at lower amounts because more people win small amounts of money than large amounts – and only five have won the top prize of £1 million.

4 a) 300

b) 150

c) 9/10ths, 90%

d) 225:100 (= 45:20) = 9:4

e) 225:50 = 9:2

f) 600

g) £1530

Accessing website links

Links to various websites are referred to throughout this BTEC Level 3 National Study Skills Guide. To ensure that these links are up-to-date, that they work and that the sites aren't inadvertently linked to any material that could be considered offensive, we have made the links available on our website: www.pearsonhotlinks.co.uk. When you visit the site, search for this title BTEC Level 3 National Study Skills Guide in Public Services or ISBN 9781846905551. From here you can gain access to the website links and information on how they can be used to help you with your studies.

Useful terms

Accreditation of Prior Learning (APL)
Some of your previous achievements and experiences may be able to be used to count towards your qualification.

Apprenticeships
Schemes that enable you to work and earn money at the same time as you gain further qualifications (an NVQ award and a technical certificate) and improve your functional skills. Apprentices learn work-based skills relevant to their job role and their chosen industry. See page 94 for information on how to access a useful website on this subject.

Assessment methods
Techniques used to check that your work demonstrates the learning and understanding required for your qualification, such as assignments, case studies and practical tasks.

Assessor
An assessor is the tutor who marks or assesses your work.

Assignment
A complex task or mini-project set to meet specific grading criteria and learning outcomes.

Awarding body
An organisation responsible for devising, assessing and issuing qualifications. The awarding body for all BTEC qualifications is Edexcel.

Credit value
The number of credits attached to your BTEC course. The credit value increases in relation to the length of time you need to complete the course, from 30 credits for a BTEC Level 3 Certificate, 60 credits for a Subsidiary Diploma, 120 credits for a Diploma, up to 180 credits for an Extended Diploma.

Degrees
Higher education qualifications offered by universities and colleges. Foundation degrees take two years to complete; honours degrees may take three years or longer.

Department for Business Innovation and Skills (BIS)
BIS is responsible for further and higher education and skills training, as well as functions related to trade and industry. See page 94 for information on how to access a useful website on this subject.

Department for Education
The Department for Education is the government department responsible for schools and education, as well as for children's services. See page 94 for information on how to access a useful website on this subject.

Distance learning
When you learn and/or study for a qualification at home or at work. You communicate with your tutor and/or the centre that organises the course by post, telephone or electronically.

Educational Maintenance Award (EMA)
An EMA is a means-tested award that provides eligible learners under 19, who are studying a full-time course at school or college, with a cash sum of money every week. See page 94 for information on how to access a useful website on this subject.

External verification
Formal checking of the programme by an Edexcel representative that focuses on sampling various assignments to check content, accurate assessment and grading.

Forbidden combinations
There are some qualifications that cannot be taken simultaneously because their content is too similar.

Functional skills
Practical skills in English, maths and ICT that enable people to work confidently, effectively and independently. Level 2 Functional Skills are mapped to the units of BTEC Level 3 National qualifications. They aren't compulsory to achieve on the course, but are of great use.

Grade boundaries

Pre-set points that determine whether you will achieve a pass, merit or distinction as the overall final grade(s) for your qualification.

Grading criteria

The specific evidence you have to demonstrate to obtain a particular grade in the unit.

Grading domains

The main areas of learning that support the learning outcomes. On a BTEC Level 3 National course these are: application of knowledge and understanding; development of practical and technical skills; personal development for occupational roles; application of PLTS and functional skills.

Grading grid

The table in each unit of your qualification specification that sets out what you have to show you can do.

Higher education (HE)

Post-secondary and post-further education, usually provided by universities and colleges.

Higher-level skills

These are skills such as evaluating or critically assessing information. They are more difficult than lower-level skills such as writing a description or making a list. You must be able to demonstrate higher-level skills to achieve a distinction.

Indicative reading

Recommended books and journals whose content is both suitable and relevant for the BTEC unit studied.

Induction

A short programme of events at the start of a course designed to give you essential information, and introduce you to your fellow learners and tutors, so that you can settle down as quickly and easily as possible.

Internal verification

The quality checks carried out by nominated tutors at your school or college to ensure that all assignments are at the right level, cover appropriate learning outcomes and grading criteria, and that all assessors are marking work consistently and to the same standard.

Investors in People (IiP)

A national quality standard that sets a level of good practice for training and developing of people within a business. Participating organisations must demonstrate commitment to achieve the standard.

Learning outcomes

The knowledge and skills you must demonstrate to show that you have effectively learned a unit.

Learning support

Additional help that is available to all learners in a school or college who have learning difficulties or other special needs.

Levels of study

The depth, breadth and complexity of knowledge, understanding and skills required to achieve a qualification, which also determines its level. Level 2 equates to GCSE level and Level 3 equates to A-level. As you successfully achieve one level, you can then progress to the next. BTEC qualifications are offered at Entry Level, then Levels 1, 2, 3, 4 and 5.

Local Education Authority (LEA)

The local government body responsible for providing education for all learners of compulsory school age. The LEA is also responsible for managing the education budget for 16–19 learners in its area.

Mandatory units

These are units that all learners must complete to gain a qualification; in this case a BTEC Level 3 National. Some BTEC qualifications have an over-arching title, eg Construction, but within Construction you can choose different pathways. Your chosen pathway may have additional mandatory units specific to that pathway.

Mentor

A more experienced person who will guide you and counsel you if you have a problem or difficulty.

Mode of delivery

The way in which a qualification is offered to learners for example, part-time, full-time, as a short course or by distance learning.

National Occupational Standard (NOS)

Statements of the skills, knowledge and understanding you need to develop in order to be competent at a particular job.

National Vocational Qualification (NVQ)

Qualifications that concentrate on the practical skills and knowledge required to do a job competently. They are usually assessed in the workplace and range from Level 1 (the lowest) to Level 5 (the highest).

Nested qualifications

Qualifications that have 'common' units, so that learners can easily progress from one to another by adding on more units

Ofqual

The public body responsible for regulating qualifications, exams and tests in England.

Optional units

Units on your course from which you may be able to make a choice. They help you specialise your skills, knowledge and understanding and may help progression into work or further education.

Pathway

All BTEC Level 3 National qualifications comprise a small number of mandatory units and a larger number of optional units. These units are grouped into different combinations to provide alternative pathways to achieving the qualification. These pathways are usually linked to different career preferences.

Peer review

This involves feedback on your performance by your peers (members of your team, or class group.) You will also be given an opportunity to review their performance.

Plagiarism

The practice of copying someone else's work, or work from any other sources (eg the internet), and passing it off as your own. This practice is strictly forbidden on all courses.

Personal, learning and thinking skills (PLTS)

The skills, personal qualities and behaviour that improve your ability to work independently. Developing these skills makes you more effective and confident at work. Opportunities for developing these skills are a feature of all BTEC Level 3 National courses. These skills aren't compulsory to achieve on the course, but are of great use to you.

Portfolio

A collection of work compiled by a learner, usually as evidence of learning, to present to an assessor.

Procrastinator

Someone who is forever putting off or delaying work, either because they are lazy or because they have poor organisational skills.

Professional body

An organisation that exists to promote or support a particular profession; for example, the Royal Institute of British Architects (RIBA).

Professional development and training

This involves undertaking activities relevant to your job to increase and/or update your knowledge and skills.

Project

A project is a comprehensive piece of work, which normally involves original research and investigation by an individual or by a team. The findings and results may be presented in writing and summarised as a presentation.

Qualifications and Credit Framework (QCF)

The QCF is a framework for recognising skills and qualifications. It does this by awarding credit for qualifications and units so that they are easier to measure and compare. All BTEC Level 3 National qualifications are part of the QCF.

Qualifications and Curriculum Development Agency (QCDA)

The QCDA is responsible for maintaining and developing the national curriculum, delivering assessments, tests and examinations and reforming qualifications.

Quality assurance

In education, this is the process of continually checking that a course of study is meeting the specific requirements set down by the awarding body.

Sector Skills Councils (SSCs)

The 25 employer-led, independent organisations responsible for improving workforce skills in the UK by identifying skill gaps and improving learning in the workplace. Each council covers a different type of industry.

Semester

Many universities and colleges divide their academic year into two halves or semesters, one from September to January and one from February to July.

Seminar

A learning event involving a group of learners and a tutor, which may be learner-led, and follow research into a topic that has been introduced at an earlier stage.

Study buddy

A person in your group or class who takes notes for you and keeps you informed of important developments if you are absent. You do the same for them in return.

Time-constrained assignment

An assessment you must complete within a fixed time limit.

Tutorial

An individual or small group meeting with your tutor at which you can discuss your current work and other more general course issues. At an individual tutorial, your progress on the course will be discussed and you can raise any concerns or personal worries you may have.

The University and Colleges Admissions Service (UCAS)

UCAS (pronounced 'you-cass') is the central organisation that processes all applications for higher education (HE) courses.

UCAS points

The number of points allocated by UCAS for the qualifications you have obtained. Higher education institutions specify how many points you need to be accepted on the courses they offer. See page 94 for information on how to access a useful website on this subject.

Unit abstract

The summary at the start of each BTEC unit that tells you what the unit is about.

Unit content

Details about the topics covered by the unit and the knowledge and skills you need to complete it.

Unit points

The number of points you gain when you complete a unit. These will depend on the grade you achieve (pass, merit or distinction).

Vocational qualification

Designed to develop knowledge and understanding relevant to a chosen area of work.

Work experience

Time you spend on an employer's premises when you learn about the enterprise, carry out work-based tasks and develop skills and knowledge.

Please note that all information given within these useful terms was correct at the time of going to print.